Standing Strong

Standing Strong

TERESA GIUDICE

with EMILY LIEBERT

GALLERY BOOKS

New York   London   Toronto   Sydney   New Delhi

G

Gallery Books
An Imprint of Simon & Schuster, Inc.
1230 Avenue of the Americas
New York, NY 10020

First Gallery Books hardcover edition October 2017

GALLERY BOOKS and colophon are registered trademarks of Simon & Schuster, Inc.

For information about special discounts for bulk purchases, please contact Simon & Schuster Special Sales at 1-866-506-1949 or business@simonandschuster.com.

The Simon & Schuster Speakers Bureau can bring authors to your live event. For more information or to book an event, contact the Simon & Schuster Speakers Bureau at 1-866-248-3049 or visit our website at www.simonspeakers.com.

Manufactured in the United States of America

10 9 8 7 6 5 4 3 2 1

Library of Congress Cataloging-in-Publication Data has been applied for.

ISBN 978-1-5011-7919-8
ISBN 978-1-5011-7920-4 (ebook)

*You taught me how to live, how to love, how
to laugh, how to dream, and how to smile.*

*You showed me how to be a mother to
my four beautiful angels and to always
thank God for all of our blessings.*

*You picked me up when I fell down, you wiped
my tears when I would cry, you were always the
first one there for me during the good times, and
the last one to leave my side during the bad.*

Everything I am or ever will be is because of you.

Without you it's not the same.

fino a quando ci incontriamo di nuovo.
Per mia madre, Antonia Gorga.
ama sempe, tua figlia Teresa

CONTENTS

And for once, you just want it to be easy.
To be simple. To be helped. To be saved.
But you know you won't be.
But you're still hoping.
And you're still wishing.
And you're still staying strong and fighting,
with tears in your eyes.
You're fighting.
—Anonymous

PROLOGUE

MY "GLAMOROUS" LIFE

*I*t was just before midnight, and I could barely keep my eyes open.

I was absolutely exhausted.

I was drained physically, emotionally, and spiritually.

I had almost no strength left.

I took two shots of espresso before leaving the house so I didn't fall asleep while driving to the airport to pick up my oldest daughter, Gia, who was returning home with her high school team after a weekend cheerleading competition in Orlando.

I'm so proud of all my daughters, but because Gia is the oldest, she's really stepped up and helped out our family in ways that no sixteen-year-old should ever have to. I was so excited to see her, even though it'd been only two days.

I blasted the radio in the car so loud it was deafening. It'd been a very long day, but then again, it seemed as if every day was just as long, a virtual repeat of the day before.

I felt like Bill Murray in the movie *Groundhog Day*.

It was as if I was running on a hamster wheel that never stopped. Around and around I went, running full speed, but I couldn't seem to get ahead. I needed a break, but I couldn't seem to catch one.

The day started for me earlier than most, about twenty-four hours prior, when my seventy-three-year-old father, who now lives with me (more on that later), came into my bedroom—not long after I'd returned home from a friend's party in Connecticut—and woke me up, asking me to take him to the hospital. He had a nosebleed that wouldn't stop *and* he was also coughing up blood. It wasn't the first time this had happened.

Before we left for the hospital, I woke up my twelve-year-old daughter, Gabriella, and told her I was putting her in charge while I was gone because I had to take Nonno to the hospital.

My poor kids.

There's always something.

It's as if we have a dark cloud hovering over our house.

I often think to myself, maybe we should move and start over. I fantasize about what life would be like if we picked up and relocated to a place like Kentucky and started from scratch. What if I was no longer Teresa Giudice, reality television star from New Jersey, and I became Teresa Smith, real estate agent from Louisville or Lexington?

What would my new house look like?

What would my new friends be like?

Where would I get my hair done?

Are there any good Italian restaurants in Kentucky?

Would the paparazzi come looking for me?

Would I be happy?

I snapped back to reality, *my* reality, not what you see on TV, as I walked into the ER with my father. As we sat in the waiting room, which was absolutely freezing, I was rubbing his back affectionately, just like he used to rub mine when I was a little girl and I was sick.

I couldn't believe I was only a few weeks away from my forty-fifth birthday. I couldn't believe I'd just buried my mother. I couldn't believe my husband was in prison. I couldn't believe that *I* went to prison.

My head hurt. My mind was racing. I was literally all over the place, both everywhere and nowhere at the same time. Is that even possible?

Recently a close friend of mine suggested that I go see someone, a therapist, to try and sort things out. I wish I had the time, but sadly I don't. And I'm not sure if I'd even know where to begin or if it would even help. Are my problems the type that can be solved by sitting across from someone for an hour every week? Lying down on some stranger's couch and telling him or her my deepest, darkest secrets. Who are they to judge me? I'm not someone who opens up easily. Or, at least I haven't been in the past. I guess I just feel like my time would be better spent getting things done for my family.

Around and around on the hamster wheel.

In addition to caring for my seventy-three-year-old father and my four young daughters, I also have to *work, work, work, work, work, work* like Rihanna to pay the bills and keep things afloat after my husband made a mess of our finances. Such a massive mess that it makes the *Exxon Valdez* oil spill seem like a glass of spilled red wine (more on that later).

And speaking of my husband . . .

While I was sitting in the ER waiting for the doctor to examine my father, I checked my phone to find a new message on CorrLinks, the email system used by inmates who are in a federal prison.

My husband, Joe, is currently serving a forty-one-month sentence, but you already know that, just like you know that I spent eleven and a half months of my life inside a federal prison camp for women in Danbury, Connecticut. (And if you didn't know that, you should read my last book, *Turning the Tables.*)

Like Frank Sinatra, my husband did it his way. And look where it got us.

So there I sat on that particular Sunday at 4:00 a.m. in the ER waiting room, reading Joe's email from late Saturday night, just a few hours before, asking me in a not-so-polite way where I was, who I was with, and what I was doing at that moment.

Was he fucking kidding me?

Well, honey, here are the answers to your email:

On Saturday, I woke up at 7:00 a.m. to get *our* girls ready for their various activities and spent the next hour driving them around and dropping them off at what felt like a million different places. Soccer, cheerleading, dance—the usual.

Then I raced home to meet my glam girls, Priscilla and Lucia, who were doing my hair and makeup for a big event that was scheduled to start around noon, where I would be doing a meet-and-greet and book signing for fans, taking pictures, hosting a Q and A, *and* a cooking demonstration all while the producers and cameras from *The Real Housewives of New Jersey* followed my every move.

By 10:00 a.m. I was in the car—a black SUV with dark-tinted windows.

I called my lawyer, Jim Leonard—who also handles a lot of my professional commitments—and screamed into the phone, "Jim, did you know I'm going to MetLife Stadium for this event today?! How many people are coming to this thing?"

"Teresa, you are so popular the only venue big enough for you was MetLife Stadium," Jim replied, being his usual sarcastic, smart-ass self.

"Seriously, what time will I be done?" I asked, because I'm always thinking about the next place I have to be. There's always a child to be dropped off or picked up. Or another work obligation.

"When you're done signing books and taking pictures," he responded. "Let's hope you're there all day. That will mean you sold a lot of books. Also, while you're there, look for Jimmy Hoffa's body; they say he's buried there somewhere."

"Goodbye," I said, rolling my eyes as I hung up.

As I sat in the back seat of the SUV, enjoying the serenity and rarity of a quiet moment, I let myself rest for a split second, tuning everything out, or at least trying to.

"Miss, can I ask you question?" the driver of the SUV asked.

"Sure," I said, prying my eyes open from what I'd hoped would be a longer moment of silence. I put on a half smile, as he met my weary gaze in his rearview mirror.

"Do you think when we stop I could take a picture with you? I would love to send it to my family and friends back home in India," he said. "They won't believe that I had a real-life movie star in my car today."

A movie star? That made me laugh.

I felt like telling him, *Buddy, if my life is a movie right now, it's a fuckin' horror movie that should be titled* What Else Could Possibly Go Wrong?

But, instead, I answered back, "Sure, although I'm not a movie star. I'm on a reality TV show."

I'm not sure he knew the difference, or even cared. He just smiled and said to me, with a big toothy grin, "Such a glamorous life you have, God bless you."

A glamorous life?

Whose?

Mine?

I can see where it may come across that way to some, but the truth is, there is nothing glitzy about my life, at least not in the last few years, and certainly not on that day as I was on my way to MetLife Stadium, completely tired.

When we arrived, my driver was very kind and helped me out of the car before we posed for a selfie together. I thanked him for getting me there safely.

I stayed at MetLife Stadium until almost 4:00 p.m. I guess that means I sold a lot of books.

Afterward I went home, quickly got changed, and ran around like a lunatic getting things in order for my seven-year-old, Audriana's, communion, which was one week away. By the time I was done with all that prep work, I had to pick up my eleven-year-old, Milania, from her friend's house before driving to my own friend's house in Connecticut. Once I got home later that night, I passed out.

Literally.

When my father woke me up at 3:00 a.m. about going to the hospital, I still had on a full face of makeup and my fake eyelashes. Miraculously, I've mastered the art of sleeping in such a way that my hair doesn't get messed up. Joe used to tell me I looked like a mummy when I was sleeping.

So you can imagine what I looked like sitting in the ER with only a few hours of sleep in me, sporting a full face of makeup, eyelashes the size of butterfly wings, and perfectly coiffed hair. *Madonna mia!*

As luck would have it, after some quick tests the doctor was able to stop my father's nosebleed and, once he'd examined him, we were sent home later in the morning.

I dropped off my father and headed back out to the supermarket to pick up chicken cutlets, raviolis, and a variety of vegetables so that I could make a nice salad to eat with our Sunday dinner around two o'clock.

By that night, I was really happy to have Gia home from Orlando—when I picked her up she was so excited to see me—and I was obviously relieved that my father didn't have to be admitted to the hospital. Unfortunately, even though we were finally all together, we would be apart again very soon, as I was scheduled to leave the next day for a week in Italy to film for *The Real Housewives of New Jersey.*

Lights, camera, DRAMA!!!

I was up bright and early the following morning, and guess where I was?

Back at the hospital with my father.

He was still coughing up blood, and now he was having trouble breathing.

They were admitting him. I was in a panic. Over the last few months I had spent so much time in hospitals, I felt like an extra on *Grey's Anatomy.*

I called Jim at 7:00 a.m. and told him, "My father is in the hospital, tell them I can't go to Italy."

Jim, always a calming force in my life when he's not busting my chops, said, "Let's give it a few hours and see how things are then. You can make up your mind a little bit later, when we have more information. How does that sound?"

I agreed.

We got off the phone and, immediately, he called Lucilla D'Agostino, the executive producer of *Real Housewives of New Jersey*, who was already in Milan with the entire production crew. Jim briefed her on the situation regarding my father.

I can only imagine how that call went.

I also reached out to my brother, Joey, and told him what was happening. He agreed to come join me so that I could leave the hospital if and when my father was stable.

When Joey got there, I said to him, "Unless Daddy is stable, I am not going anywhere."

He took one look at me and asked, "Teresa, did you get any sleep?"

"I don't have time to sleep," I replied—a statement that just about sums up my world right now.

Welcome to my (not so) glamorous life.

I'm about to get *very* real. More than I ever have before. No holding back. No glossing over. No smiling through the pain. I'm digging deep, opening up, and putting it *all* out there. I'm spilling my true feelings about what's gone down in the last couple of years.

It's my time to speak up.

1

KNOCKED DOWN BUT NOT OUT

Let's get one thing straight. I didn't go to camp. I went to prison. The big house. The clink. The pokey. Call it what you want, but you get the picture. I know I've referred to it as camp in the past, but honestly, it was nothing like that.

It was a living hell.

An absolute nightmare.

So, why did I sugarcoat it?

You want the truth? I couldn't believe I was in prison. That's right. I still don't believe it. I thought that just by saying the word "prison," it would somehow validate it, make it real. Trust me: it was real. Every second of every minute of every hour of every day of every fucking month I sat in that horrible place, away from my home, away from my family. Maybe I'm superstitious. I know that may sound silly, but camp sounded so much better. So much softer and easier to explain, especially for my little ones, Milania and Audriana. I asked my friends and family to use the same word, too.

Still, despite my time spent at the federal correctional institution in Danbury, Connecticut, I know in my heart that I'm not a criminal. I will never accept that label, because it's not who I am. It's simply just not me.

I remember the day that Joe and I were sentenced like it was yesterday. After we got home from court, I went upstairs to my bedroom, shut the door, and cried. I couldn't digest it. Did that really just happen? I heard my door open and in walked my mother. She saw me crying, so she took my head and gently lowered it to her chest. She said, "Only God can judge you. He knows who you are and what you are." And, like always, my mom was right.

So I don't care what people say or what they think. I really don't. They only know what they read in the tabloids, see on the Internet, or what they watch on TV. What's that saying? *Why let the truth get in the way of a good story?* Well, I guess that's what happened with me. People got so caught up in the drama of it, my rise and fall, my plummet from the top, my harsh new reality, that they ignored the actual facts of what really happened. But I know my own truth, as do those who love and support me. And, most important, God knows.

Before this entire legal nightmare started, Joe and I were on top of the world, or so it seemed to me.

We were living in our gorgeous, ten-thousand-plus-square-foot custom-built home on four acres, complete with waterfalls and fishponds, with our four beautiful daughters, Gia, Gabriella, Milania, and Audriana.

Joe's construction businesses were successful, and I was staying home to raise the kids.

I was a *real* New Jersey housewife long before I became one on television. We didn't have any financial concerns, at least none that I knew of. So, for me, it felt like one day we were riding high and then the next day we got knocked down.

But not knocked out.

Never that.

Despite it all, I am still standing, standing strong.

What choice do I have?

People will screw you. Especially when you're on top. I've definitely learned that the hard way, and so have my husband and children. Practically overnight we became targets, walking bull's-eyes, and we didn't even know it. I was so naive and, looking back, Joe was so stupid.

When I first signed up for *Real Housewives*, I specifically asked Joe, "Is everything good with you and your businesses, you know, financially?" And he said, "Yeah, everything is fine. You want to do the show? Do it."

So, that's what made me move forward. I didn't think anything else of it. I figured, they're just going to follow me and my friends doing what we normally do. Going shopping, eating out for lunch and dinner, working out, whatever. I never thought it would lead to us getting into any trouble. Because, if I did, or if I knew that my husband was doing something illegal, I never would have signed up in a million years. Or, if he would have told me not to do it, I would have listened.

To this day, he still claims he didn't know he was doing anything wrong, and I'm not going to lie, that really pisses me off. He says he thought that his accountant was filing our taxes. Really? But Joe didn't check things! That's what makes me so upset. You have to be on top of your shit, and he wasn't. Dot your i's and cross your t's. For my part, all I did was sign some paperwork. I went to two closings for two different properties, with lawyers, a mortgage broker, and a real estate broker, and signed in front of them, so I thought it was fine. I had to be the one to sign because Joe was using my credit, since it was so good. He was planning to flip the homes. But that was all I did. I was never involved in his business. Nothing. Hello? What would I know about construction? I would say, "Do I have to sign any tax returns?" Because I was used to signing tax returns every year when I worked. "No," he'd say. "No, *everything is fine*. You don't work anymore." So, I didn't think anything further about it. I just listened to whatever he said. I trusted him. He's my husband. He was taking care of all the bills. I was just a housewife taking care of the house and cooking dinner every night. That was my job. Even though I'd originally planned to go back to work in the fashion industry after I had Gia, I decided it was more important for me to be at home to raise my children. That was what my mom did when Joey and I were growing up. And we loved having her there for us. We ate dinner as a family together every single night. I wanted to replicate that for my own kids.

Most people would have paid a fine, learned their lesson, and never made the same mistake again.

But not me. I think they wanted to make an example of me because I'm famous. Actually, that's exactly what they did. The thing is, to be taken away from your family, to me that's just trying to punish someone. And, in the end, the ones who were really punished were my children. I remember one of the US attorneys saying, "Kids are resilient; they'll be fine with it." How could he say that? What kids would be fine with both their parents going to prison? They were the ones who suffered for eleven and a half months while I was away and are now suffering all over again with their father gone for forty-one months. No child should have to go through that. It's not like we killed or even hurt anyone.

I'll never forget a case that happened in the federal courts up in North Jersey after ours. It received a ton of media attention, certainly more than ours did. The media called it "Bridgegate," and it involved allegations that various individuals who worked closely with New Jersey governor Chris Christie took steps to shut down a portion of the George Washington Bridge that serves as a major connector between New Jersey and New York. It was all in an effort to punish the mayor of Fort Lee, New Jersey, who had allegedly somehow pissed off the governor.

Anyway, there ends up being a trial, and one of the people who was convicted was a woman named Bridget Kelly, who once worked for the governor. She received a sentence of eighteen months in prison. What bothered me most about this story was the fact that this woman was a single mother of four young children and she was going to prison.

The governor, her former boss, was never charged.

That's justice?

People say that I didn't take accountability for what I did. But you know what? I did. In fact, I took the blame for something I *didn't* do. And I served my time, quietly. I took my punishment. I went. I kept my mouth shut. I did what I had to do.

My thing is, I'm very strong. You've got to just pick yourself up, deal with it, and move on. You've got to put your head down and keep going forward. What else are you going to do? Cry about it? I did it for my kids. I kept it all together the best I could. Look, I had my moments—who wouldn't? But even when I wasn't there for my children physically, I still had control over what was going on around the house, or I tried to.

Joe didn't deal with it as well as I did. Shortly before I left, he lost his father, with whom he was very close. We all were. That was an extremely difficult time for him, especially because it happened so unexpectedly. His dad was a healthy man, and then, one day, he dropped dead on the side of our house, near where Joe kept some chickens in a coop. After Joe's father passed away, he lost me to prison. He never voiced the extent of his pain to me, which I wish he would have, but I know that's a result of his upbringing. Joe doesn't talk about things that bother him; he thinks it makes him look weak. He likes to be the strong man. Only he wasn't that strong. He drowned his sorrows in alcohol from the day we were sentenced to the day he left for prison. All the kids and I saw was his drinking too much, all the time. He was constantly drunk. I guess that was the way he coped. At the time it pissed me off; now it makes me sad. Still, my family didn't see me drinking, because I wasn't. I was the one holding it all together.

Someone had to.

When it was Joe's turn to start his sentence, I knew exactly what his daily life was going to be like. Sadly, he did not. I didn't feel sorry for him, though, not for one second. I know that might sound cold or harsh, but it's the truth. I did my time, and now he has to do his. He was the one who got us into all this bullshit in the first place. He can blame me all he wants, which he does, very often. He says that none of it ever would have happened if we weren't on the show, which is because of me, but I know that's not true. It was his fault, because he didn't do things correctly. And now he's paying for his bad judgment. We're *all* paying for it.

Sometimes I wish Joe would man up and say, "I'm sorry, I know I fucked up," but he doesn't. And that's not cool with me.

Despite blaming Joe, the three months between when I got home and when Joe left was a happy time for our family, except for Joe's constant and obsessive drinking. I was thrilled to be back where I belonged, with my husband and my girls, and they were so excited to have me back. It's not easy for a mother to be away from her family. I'd always been the one to handle everything for the kids. Joe couldn't even drive! His license was suspended because of another one of his screwups, and even though I tried my best to stay in control of the goings-on in my house while I was gone, it wasn't the same as having me there. All kids need their moms, especially girls. Actually, kids need both their parents, but that's another story.

Joe told me that when I got home it was a load off everyone's shoulders but that it sucked knowing that time was running out for him and that we were going to have to go through another horrible goodbye all over again. He said he was mesmerized by me for those three months and that my being away made him realize how much he really loved his wife and kids. He told me that even though my parents and his sister-in-law helped him out (a lot!), four kids is exhausting. No shit, honey! I wanted to punch him in his face when he said that. He finally appreciated everything I'd been doing for so long?! Too little too late.

During those three months, Joe also said that he felt like a little puppy following me around. He just wanted to spend as much time with me as possible before his long journey ahead. He didn't know what prison was going to be like, and the thought of leaving us for so long was unspeakable. I felt like saying, *Hello, I know! I did it!* But, you know what? I got through it and I know he will as well.

In the final weeks leading up to Joe's leaving, he was really trying to get stuff in order for the house. He dealt with plumbers, electricians, landscapers—you name it. Four acres requires a lot of upkeep. Before he left, he was also having a lot of lunches with his friends. They all wanted to take him out to eat and drink, which is understandable. I mean, my friends wanted to do that with me, too.

I think he was anxious about going, but he wasn't expressing it to me, because he's old-school like that. He doesn't show emotion. I really feel like he didn't open up enough to me, which I think he should have. I wanted him to. But that's sort of the way our relationship is. He doesn't like to express his feelings about things. And life was so busy with the kids and filming the show. Things just kind of moved along as usual, until the night before Joe was scheduled to leave for prison.

I had hoped that last night would be nice and quiet for our family.

I had hoped that Joe and the girls and I would get to spend some alone time together.

Boy, was I wrong!

The night before Joe left, *everyone* was at our house. He has such a big family, and there's no saying no to them. They just show up and stay. I was annoyed, because I wanted alone time with my husband. And I felt like it was unfair that I couldn't have that. I mean, I'm his wife. He has four daughters. We needed more time with him. He wasn't going to see us for three years. Three years!

Even though we had those three months together when I came home from prison, it wasn't enough, especially since I had to start working right away. All I wanted to do was rush into my house for the first time in eleven and a half months, hug and kiss my babies, and then take a very long, very hot shower; get in my pajamas; and climb into my huge bed with a zillion pillows and sleep for a week.

I did pull Joe aside that last night and say, "When I left, we had alone time. You know my family's not like your family. It's like they don't get that we're not going to be alone together for a really long time. They should give us space. They're not here with you every day. I'm here with you every day."

I was upset for the kids, too, but they seemed to be fine with it. They love having people over. They're used to us always having company at our house. I just thought we deserved more attention from Joe.

At one point, all four of my girls were in the bed with me while the party went on downstairs. One of the producers from *Real Housewives*, Caroline Self, came in to my house and up to my bedroom to check on me. We weren't even working that night. I was very touched by her kindness. She didn't need a Harvard degree (which she has) to sense that something wasn't right, with everyone downstairs drinking and me and the girls upstairs in my bedroom. Ya think?

Once the girls had gone to sleep, Joe and his family and more than a dozen of his closest friends remained downstairs in my kitchen, drinking Joe's homemade red wine, laughing, and having what sounded like a good old time, while I stayed upstairs in my bedroom, crying, by myself, knowing that I was going to be saying my own goodbye to him the next day. For what felt like forever.

Finally, Joe came upstairs and we stayed up even later, trying to make the night last as long as we could. We had sex for the last time. But, eventually, exhaustion took over and we couldn't stay up any longer. I literally cried myself to sleep. Joe passed out next to me; he was drunk, as usual.

The next morning, Joe and I were both up early to get Gia, Gabriella, and Audriana off to school. Milania is very close with Joe, so she begged us to stay home until he left, and we both agreed to let her.

Watching Joe say goodbye to Gia, Gabriella, and Audriana as they left for school with tears in their eyes broke my heart. I couldn't help but ask myself, *How did we get to this point? Is this really my life? Is there a reason why this is happening to us?* I couldn't believe what was going on. I was always such a good girl growing up. I never did anything wrong. And now my family was entangled in this nightmare. At this point, my time in prison seemed like such a distant memory, even though I had been home for only about ninety days. Now my poor girls were going through it all over again. I felt sick for them and for myself.

Joe was scheduled to turn himself in at FCI Fort Dix at 12:00 p.m. sharp on March 23, 2016, so he had to leave our house no later than 9:30 a.m. to make it there on time. At first, I wasn't even going to go with him, because he didn't come with me when I went. Just my lawyer, Jim Leonard, took me. I thought that would be easier and less emotional for both Joe and me. Also, it was supposed to be only guys taking Joe—his brother, Pete; his cousin Ralph; his uncle Dimitri; and a few others. But then his sister, Maria, said she was going, so I decided to go, too. I knew it would be hard and awkward saying goodbye with everyone there, but I had no choice. No one would leave us alone! Again, there's no privacy when it comes to Joe's family.

Joe's brother was scheduled to drive, and he arrived shortly after the girls went off to school. Then came Joe's sister and his uncle and his cousin. Before I knew it, my kitchen was filled once again with our family and friends. They drank three bottles of wine, a bottle of champagne, and a bottle of Johnnie Walker Blue—in the morning, before most people had their breakfast! Joe said he was eating and drinking like he was going to prison, which obviously he was! Duh! I was walking around my house in a daze. I couldn't believe that he was getting ready to leave in less than an hour and here he was sitting in the kitchen drinking, telling his jokes, and being the life of the party while I was dying on the inside and Milania was sitting on his lap hugging him and quietly crying as she rested her head on his shoulder.

At one point, my brother, Joey, and our attorney, Jim, both came up to me and asked me if I was okay, and I remember telling them that I was numb. I had so much I wanted to talk to Joe about before he left and, now that he was actually going, I barely had five minutes alone with him.

As we were getting ready to leave, all the producers from

Real Housewives who had been waiting respectfully outside the house, giving us a little bit of privacy, asked Jim if they could come in and say their goodbyes to Joe. One by one they came inside, hugged Joe, and then made their way to me to do the same. It was touching to see that most of them had tears in their eyes. These are the people who are in our house day in and day out, and they've become like members of our family, even though a lot of times we are fighting with them (especially Joe, and even Milania, who calls them "the Filmers").

Joe's brother, Pete, broke up "the party" by saying, "Come on, Joe, we need to get going." And then Joe poured everyone a shot of Johnnie Walker Blue and made a toast in Italian that translated to: "To family, friends; to good health and freedom." The kitchen got very quiet, and I noticed most of the men had tears in their eyes. The only thing that cut the silence was their muffled sniffles. One at a time, Joe's friends started going up to him and saying their goodbyes, embracing him tight, whispering something to him, and kissing him on his cheek. It was heart-wrenching and reminded both of us of the same horrible feelings we had when I left. At least then, it was only Joe and me in the kitchen, as the girls were all asleep, and Jim, who was driving me to Danbury, went outside to give us some privacy.

I wished that someone would have done that for me on this day. I really wanted to be alone with my husband, even if just for five minutes, but I never got the chance.

By this point, the paparazzi had formed outside of our gate, and we did our best to shield ourselves from them as Joe and I got into Pete's black Lincoln Navigator to follow Jim to Fort Dix. Joe saw Milania crying in the window, and he said that was torture for him. It was for me, too. I knew exactly how he felt. The image of tucking my girls into bed before going to prison for eleven and a half months is something I will never forget, though I wish I could.

Sadly, there is a lot I wish I could forget.

As we drove down the driveway, the paparazzi rushed Pete's car in an attempt to snap pictures of Joe and me, so they could sell them to the gossip magazines, but Joe's sister, Maria, shielded us with her jacket. We followed Jim down the road. Some people were talking and trying to keep the mood upbeat, but I was mostly quiet in the car, holding hands with Joe but not saying much. Looking back, I now realize that Joe and I didn't communicate well with each other in our marriage, all too often not saying things that needed to be said. Joe is someone who doesn't like to talk about things. He holds things close to the vest.

On the way to the prison, Joe wanted Burger King for his last meal, so we stopped there. Fucking Burger King, can you imagine? I wasn't hungry at all. As a matter of fact, I was sick to my stomach and couldn't believe he wanted to eat at a time like that, but prison food is disgusting, and to each their own, I guess. He probably wanted something to absorb all the liquor he'd consumed.

Before I knew it, we were approaching the Fort Dix Air Force base in South Jersey, which also houses the prison complex where Joe was scheduled to report. As we went through the security checkpoint, two prison vehicles were traveling with us, one in front of Jim's car and one behind Pete's car. Ultimately, they directed us to an empty parking lot, where the guards told Joe that he should say his final goodbyes.

He went around and greeted everyone with hugs and kisses, until he got to me last. Joe held me tighter than he ever had before and said, "I love you, honey. Take care of the kids." Then he kissed me (it wasn't like we could make out or anything!), and I could see that he was crying. I wasn't crying anymore. For one, I was all cried out. Also, I remembered when Jim dropped me off at prison and I just said, "Okay, goodbye. I've got this. I'll do it." Not to mention that part of me felt relieved that Joe was finally starting his sentence. I knew that the sooner he started, the sooner this nightmare would be over once and for all.

Once we'd said goodbye, the two guards escorted Joe to a building that looked like an old elementary school about a hundred yards from us, as we all stood there watching him walk away. He turned around one time and gave us a wave, but before I could blink, my husband was gone, disappearing into that building to begin serving his forty-one-month sentence.

That was the moment I realized I was a single mother and that it was my responsibility to raise our four girls by myself.

It was like I was staring into an abyss. I was now all alone.

I later found out that after we left and Joe checked in, the guards didn't take him to his room all day because he kept blowing the highest alcohol level on their device. Then he had to go to the medical department for five hours to sober up. It wasn't until 7:00 p.m. that they let him in and gave him some food, a toothbrush, soap, and sneakers. He said the whole thing felt surreal and that all he could think about was when he would get to go home, and when he would be able to call his family—which wasn't until the next day. He said that drove him nuts not to hear our voices. He met a few nice guys, including Apollo Nida, Phaedra Parks's ex from *The Real Housewives of Atlanta*, and basically tried to keep busy just like I had.

I understood what he was going through, but—again—I didn't feel sorry for him. I'd already served my time.

The ride back was sad. Unlike the way there, nobody talked in the car. When I got back to our house, I went straight to my bedroom and rested there until the kids got home from school. I don't think I cried anymore. I was just thinking, *Oh my God, I can't believe I've got to do this by myself now.* Even though I was totally fine with him going, because I had to go, too—and I knew that if I could do it, he could do it—I still had to digest that I had a tremendous amount of responsibility I had to look forward to as a single parent.

Once the kids came home from school, we all had an early dinner together and picked up right where we left off. That's what we do. We have a family dinner before their after-school activities—I usually cook—then they have a little snack afterward. I do homework with Audriana and sometimes Milania. And then they take showers and get ready for bed. That's our everyday life. On Sundays, we have a big Italian dinner in the afternoon. All the kids have to be there, and they can't leave the table until everyone is finished eating—just like when I was a kid. My father was and still is a stickler for that!

Of course the girls did ask how it went dropping Joe off, and I said everything went well. I told them that as soon as Daddy can call us he will, and as soon as he gets situated, we'll go see him. They felt good about that.

Sadly, having a parent behind bars had now become a part of their routine. At bedtime, Milania and Audriana got teary-eyed again and said that they missed Daddy. I just comforted them by saying, "Daddy will be home soon. Look at Mommy—I'm home now. It went so quick, right?" Audriana was only in first grade when Joe left, so I told her Daddy went to work, but the other girls knew what was really going on.

The positive side is that things definitely got easier for the girls when I got home, especially for Gia, which I was happy about. She shouldered much more responsibility when Joe was home and I was away. And she deserves to be a kid. I want her to enjoy life.

The next day we got right back into things. When something's new, you just have to push yourself through it. You have to say to yourself, *I'm okay. I can do this.* What other choice is there?

At first, I was truly good with Joe being gone and doing everything by myself, because I was used to it to some extent. And we got to talk to Joe that day; it was a relief to know he was okay. He sounded upbeat. The kids didn't cry. They were so happy to hear from him. They said, "Daddy, we love you!" over and over.

We saw him for the first time about two weeks later. Even though Fort Dix is in New Jersey, it's about two hours away. We all cried when we first saw him. He's in a room with twelve guys, which is crazy. Some of them are pedophiles and child molesters. Joe told me that really grosses the guys out. They call them "chomos" for short! Shortly after our visit, one of the inmates in his room got chicken pox and they locked them down for twenty-one days, which drove Joe crazy.

I knew Joe would make friends. I wasn't worried about that. He's a friendly guy, and everyone always loves him. And I knew he would have plenty of visitors. Except my dad. My dad and Joe were very close. They played cards together and talked a lot. Still, my dad never even came to see me. I thought maybe it was because it would be too hard for him to see me in prison, although I never really understood why. I just accepted it. But, recently, he told me that the reason he never came was because he couldn't go there without taking me home with him. He said it would have been too painful for him to leave me there, and I know it would be the same for him with Joe. My mom came to visit me when I was incarcerated. (She was still waiting for approval to go see Joe when she passed away.) I felt badly because she wasn't feeling well. One time she came with a cane. It was from her rheumatoid arthritis. I was heartbroken, because she was so young and I'd never seen her need assistance walking before!

Part of me blames myself. While I was away, she was helping raise my four daughters. And her rheumatoid arthritis was taking over her joints. I'm sure she suffered inside because she was upset about what happened to me. It was embarrassing for my parents. They're Italian—straight off the boat, goes the saying—so having their daughter and son-in-law go to prison was unheard of for them. They know it wasn't something that I did. Regardless, it took its toll.

It takes a toll on all of us. I miss Joe. I think about what he's doing there. What his days are like. The girls miss their father, too. They know Daddy isn't here for a while, much longer than Mommy. I know they had to grow up quickly through all of this, but I always try to look at the bright side. Of course, I couldn't believe I had to go away. I really couldn't. But I could have been killed in a car crash. And they would never have gotten me back. I don't know if they get that right now, but I think in a way it will help them in life in the future. At the moment, they feel like they have the worst circumstances. They can't believe that their mother had to go away, and then their father. Like my parents, it's embarrassing for them, too. But, listen, every family goes through things. When I hear stories from other people, of their hardships, I say, "Please go tell Gia your story, so she knows she's not the only one who's going through something difficult."

I thought we had the perfect life. I really did. Until this bullshit happened.

Now all I do is work to provide for my kids, the best I can. I feel guilty when I have to be gone for long hours. Or when I have to get a babysitter. They could have been home with their father! But he's not here, and no one else is helping me. I'm doing it all on my own. I'm driving the kids everywhere, doing everything for everyone. My parents were here every day to help Joe while I was away. I don't even have my mom anymore. And my dad isn't well. As I said, he currently lives with us.

The bottom line is that the kids need two parents. They need both of us. And, now, on top of doing everything, I also have to be Mom *and* Dad to my girls. Sometimes they don't want to be part of the show; actually, *most* times they don't want to be part of the show. They would rather lead normal lives away from the spotlight, but there's nothing I can do. This is how I make my living.

This is the price I pay to keep my family afloat.

2

NEW BEGINNINGS

One good thing that came from my time in prison was that it healed my relationship with my brother, Joey, and helped strengthen my relationship with my sister-in-law Melissa. My mother and father both said there was nothing worse than witnessing their kids fighting the way we did. *Madonna mia* did we fight! The day before I left for Danbury, Joey called me and we really had it out. But, eventually, time healed our wounds. He visited me while I was in prison and, when he came, it was as if we'd never missed a beat. He was my baby brother all over again. Despite everything that we had been through, I loved him and he loved me.

Not many people know this but my lawyer, Jim, also represents Joey and Melissa. He would come and see me while I was at Danbury and tell me how important it was to "make things right" with them before I came home. He would listen to my side of things, and I'm sure their side as well, and he would look at me and say, "Forget about the show. Forget about the media. Who gives a fuck what other people think? Do it for your parents. Do it for the kids. Do it for your family." And he was right. I just wasn't ready. It was me being stubborn.

Like, with Melissa, she tried to visit me in prison, but I was still too angry with her for everything that had happened between us. I was thinking, *Uh-uh, sorry, you're not coming to see me. You should have been nice to me while I was home.* I kept saying she didn't get approved, but the truth was that at that time, I really had no desire to be in her presence, especially considering where I was. Jim would ask me, "Is Melissa approved yet? She wants to come see you," and I would tell him, "I'm working on it," and he would say, "Seems like you're really working hard on it," and I would laugh. But it is what it is.

That being said, when I came home, I did forgive Melissa, and we picked up right where we left off before she and Joey joined the show. That's the way I always wanted it. I tried to forget everything that ever happened. Well, almost everything.

To me, family is the most important thing. I'm very old-school. I'm like *The Godfather* movie. You never go against family. And when you do, it's ugly, and God doesn't like ugly. I try to teach my daughters that, because what upset me the most about the situation with my brother was that my kids and his kids saw us fighting. So, now, when I tell them not to fight with one another, it doesn't carry as much weight because of the example we set.

Even though things got better between me and Joey and Melissa once I got home, there was and still is a lot of tension between my brother and my husband. Joe and Joey used to be very close. Joey looked up to Joe like a big brother, but he blames my husband for what happened to us. He thinks it's all his fault, and that I never should have gone to prison. Joey knows who I am. He knows that I never got in any trouble before this, ever. I mean, my parents were angry at Joe, too. They voiced it to me, but never to him, which I think is amazing. Of course Joe's mother thinks it happened because we were on the show and blames me, which isn't right. She's in denial about her son and what he did. Who knows? Maybe I'd be the same way with my own kids.

Anyway, by the time season seven was beginning to roll around, I was so ready to be done with all the drama.

One time when Jim came to see me at Danbury, I handed him two notes, one for Melissa and one for my fellow New Jersey housewife Jacqueline Laurita.

The note to Melissa read:

Melissa,
Looking forward to Christmas Eve with our family, should I
bring sprinkle cookies?
Love, love, love U
xoxox
Teresa

The note to Jacqueline read:

Jacqueline,
Heard you were asking about me, we have a lot to catch up
on. Looking forward to a new beginning.
xoxoxo
Teresa

And the truth is, I was looking for new beginnings with both of them, but Melissa more so than Jacqueline. That said, Jacqueline and I do have a lot of history with each other and not all of it is bad. At one time she was one of my closest friends, or so I thought.

Regardless, I knew I was going to have to work with both of them, so I wanted things to be as good as possible. I also learned that Siggy Flicker and Dolores Catania were joining the cast. I didn't know Siggy, but she ended up being a total sweetheart. The first thing she announced that season was that she'd had a facelift, as she sipped lobster bisque from a straw! My kind of girl!

Dolores had been on other seasons, but we were all trying to get her on permanently. I've known Dolores for more than twenty years—she's very close with Dina Manzo, who used to be on the show and is still one of my best friends and Audriana's godmother. Dolores is one tough cookie, which I like. Even tougher than I am! Viewers haven't seen the full extent of that yet, but trust me, they will.

Of course, while I was happy to be home with my daughters and back to work, I also had to say goodbye to Joe, which made this particular season very difficult for me.

Fortunately, the producers were very respectful and didn't push coming inside the house, except to say their own farewells to Joe. They shot us outside, because we didn't want to wear mics. I told them, "This is a private time for us. I need to be with my husband, friends, and family, so I don't want you guys in the house." I said, "You got me when I came home." A lot of people said they couldn't believe I let them do that, but I allowed it—even though I wanted to curl up in bed with my daughters—because that was a joyous day for our family, so why not?

I feel like I've still yet to have my aha moment or an awesome season. When I first started the show, I didn't have time to take pleasure in it. It was the very beginning, and everything was so foreign to me. Then, after that, families joined the show, which added new complications. And, after that, there was all the legal stuff we went through. I'm still waiting for a season where I can just sit back and enjoy. I'm hoping eight will be my lucky number!

Still, season seven was a change for me because of all I'd been through and was still going through, though my motto was *I'm just gonna leave the past in the past and look to a brighter future.*

I'd never been in any legal trouble before, so I truly didn't understand what was going on. It was so sad because I felt like everybody else knew what was going on except me. When you're in the public eye, you get punished. I was very naive about the process. Now, I know. I've learned so much from all of this.

I'll tell you one thing, if I'd known what I know now, I never would have spent all that money on legal fees. It would give me great pleasure to help anyone else who has to go through what I went through, because maybe things would work out differently for them. I wanted to go to trial, but I was told that if you go to trial and you lose, you get an even worse punishment, like two or three times worse than if you just take a plea deal. That's important, and people don't get that. Until you've walked in those shoes, you don't entirely understand how the legal system works, or at least I didn't. Even my husband was green to the whole process. So I felt like we spent unnecessary money. If I'd known what I know now, I would have just taken a plea deal from day one and saved my family a lot of aggravation and a lot of money. Money that could have gone toward paying off restitution or been deposited into our kids' college funds. It kills me to think about it.

I remember Jim telling me at Danbury, "Teresa, the United States government prints their own money and fights world wars, what chance did you and Joe have against them?"

In other words, it was over before it started, and sadly, he was right. We never had a chance.

Now, I get that no one's perfect, and that everyone does make mistakes. Hell, I used to think I was perfect, but nope, not even close. I've learned that people do all sorts of things they never imagined they'd do. For example, they cheat on their spouses and then forgive each other. I used to say that if Joe cheated on me, that would be the end of our relationship, which is still the truth. But now I realize that I have the right to feel that way, even though someone else might feel differently. To each his own, you know what I mean? I'm not in that person's marriage. What works for them and their family, may not make sense for me and my family.

I have a new outlook on life since I came back from prison and since I took up yoga as a discipline. A few seasons ago, I remember telling Melissa on camera, "God forgives, I don't," and she looked at me like I was a crazy person. In retrospect, it does sound kind of crazy. Still, there are things and certain people I will never forgive, and Jacqueline is one of them. I would never have done anything—nor would I ever do anything—as malicious as the things Jacqueline did to me. She intended to hurt me, and as a result, she hurt my family. She manipulated and schemed behind the scenes, stirring the pot the whole time. She is a master at that. I gave her a lot of freaking chances, and in the end, the things she did were unforgivable. I won't rehash them, but everyone saw most of it on the show.

She also turned my family against me for a period of time, although Melissa can't stand her now, too. I forgave Joey and Melissa.

It was hard to be knocked down by people I thought cared about me. Even Caroline Manzo and her family kicked me while I was down. I stood on my own two feet, though, all by myself. I took all the beatings that came at me, and I was stronger for it.

Once filming of season seven wrapped, I was so relieved. I finally felt like I could relax, and I was really looking forward to the summer. I was just concentrating on my family. The end of the school year was approaching, which is always a very busy time for my girls. I wanted to focus on my daughters, and I also wanted to finally start thinking about getting certified as a yoga instructor.

When I was in prison, I'd been working out hard at the gym and lifting heavy weights all the time. It was my way of distracting myself, of keeping the boredom at bay, and of trying to improve myself all at once. I loved it. But, my roommate kept telling me, "You get out of bed like an old person," because I was always so sore from the weight lifting. My lower back was killing me. That's when I decided to try one of the yoga classes they offered. I'd done it before at home and didn't think it was for me, but I had nothing better to do with my time! And, you know what, I started feeling so good. It was a lot of stretching, and it really transformed my body. I never got sick of it. It releases so many wonderful endorphins. I even started meditating because of yoga.

As much as it was changing my body, it was also changing my mind.

I wanted to learn everything I could about it. I said, "Maybe eventually I'll teach." Also, because of my passion for and experience in the fashion world, I've always thought I could design a line of activewear. In the back of my mind, I'm constantly thinking about business and new ways to support my family. I have to.

I need to work. I need to provide for myself and for my kids.

I began the certification process when I first got home from prison, but I had to stop because when we're filming, it takes over our whole lives. For example, if there's an 11:00 a.m. call time, I have to get ready right after I get my kids to school, and then once we actually begin filming, it can go on for hours.

There's a yoga studio two minutes from my house. Originally, I was just taking classes there, and then I found out they offered certification programs, so I figured it was meant to be. In the beginning, there were about fifteen of us doing it together. That was when I dropped out, because the show was taking up too much of my time. I started, but I couldn't complete it. When I went back to it, it was only four of us and it was during the day—Tuesdays and Thursdays from nine to two— which was great for me and one other mom who had children in school. Then there was one other lady and a man, who was a retired cop. I have to say it was pretty awesome. Audriana has gotten into yoga, too. I've taken her to a yoga studio for children and she loves it.

I also told Joe he should do it! He's really flexible—which I'm not—because he's a black belt. You know that actor guy, Jean-Claude Van Damme, who does martial arts, and he does splits across two chairs or something. My husband can do that—we even have a photo! You wouldn't necessarily think that of Joe, because he got so big from lifting weights, but I think yoga would be right up his alley. Being bulky isn't in anymore. A trim, toned body is what's in.

That's one of the reasons I'm happy Joe went away. He's losing tons of weight in prison. He's not drinking alcohol, and he's eating a lot less since the food is horrible. Like I did, all he does is work out in there. I tell him, "You want to be lean and cut." He will be.

I think he'll do yoga with me when he gets home. As I said, it goes hand in hand with his black belt. They're both disciplines that teach focus.

So, anyway, I wrapped filming for season seven in April 2016, and when that happens, my days are very different. I get up at six thirty in the morning. I make myself coffee and breakfast for me and Gia. Then I'll prepare lunches for Gia, Milania, and Audriana—typically leftover chicken cutlets, or a turkey or tuna sandwich. Gabriella likes to pack her own lunch because she's into being healthy. I order her these peanut butter crepes that she's really into right now. Or she'll wash and cut up her own fruit—blueberries, grapes, strawberries, and sometimes mangoes.

At seven o'clock, I drive Gia to the high school, because she starts earlier than the other girls. Then I get back home around seven fifteen or so, make the other girls breakfast, and finish helping Milania and Audriana get ready—they're both in elementary school—and I drive them to their building around 7:50, for an 8:10 start. After that, I go home again, have another cup of coffee, make sure Gabriella is ready, and finally I drive Gabriella to school around eight fifteen because her day begins at eight thirty. It's very busy!!

Once the house is empty, I'll straighten up a little bit, get dressed, and head to a nine-fifteen yoga class, which is usually over by eleven. After that, I'll meet my friends for lunch or run errands. I always try to be home by three o'clock, because that's when the girls get off the bus—they like to be driven to school in the morning, but take the bus home. By that time, they're starving, so we do our early dinner, activities, homework, showers, and bed.

I promise you that my life outside of the show is not fancy. We're all just doing what's necessary to get by. I have no husband to help me. My mother is gone. I'm in this alone. That's why when people—former cast members, friends who I thought I could trust, and even random haters—try to sabotage my family, I lose my mind. They don't understand what we go through every day.

They don't even know us.

3

HAPPY BIRTHDAY TO ME?

*M*ay is always a big month in our family. First comes Mother's Day; then my birthday, on May 18; and then Joe's birthday, on May 22. What I didn't know is that 2016 would be the last Mother's Day with my mom. It's still hard for me to even think about that, let alone write those words.

I spent the day with my mom and my family at my house. We had our usual Sunday Italian dinner in the afternoon. Mother's Day is always a special day for us, because my mom was the rock of our family, so we loved celebrating her. I said to her, "Let's go out to dinner," but I don't think she wanted to, because restaurants can be very busy and she preferred to just hang out at home and be with my father and me and the girls. I always asked my mom to pick out something she wanted for a gift. I loved being able to buy her nice things, even though she wasn't into expensive clothing or makeup.

I think it's important to feel appreciated by your children on Mother's Day. I know my kids always make me feel that way. That year felt extra special because I'd been in prison the previous year and everyone was so glad to have me home.

Audriana wrote me this beautiful letter, which meant so much to me.

> *My mom is the best mom in the whole world. One reason*
> *is that she is kind, because she brings me what I need*
> *to school. Another reason is that she is nice because she*
> *makes me breakfast. She is terrific because she gets me*
> *Pokémon and Barbies. Also, another reason is that she is*
> *awesome because she lets me do anything I want. Another*
> *reason is that she is excellent because she neatens my*
> *clothes. And, the last reason is that she is loving because*
> *she gives.*

Milania recorded a video for me in which she said:

> *Happy Mother's Day, Mom, I love you so much. I love you*
> *because you're so kind and loving and you help me when I'm*
> *sad and you cheer me up. I love you so much. You are just so*
> *amazing and you're the best mom ever! I love you, Mommy.*
> *Happy Mother's Day.*

Gia posted an old photo of us holding hands on the red car-
pet, with the caption:

*Happy Mother's Day to my best friend! Thank you for
always being by my side and never failing to make me
smile! I love you!*

I love receiving handmade gifts from my girls or senti-
ments like those, because they come from the heart. It was an
emotional day, in a good way, because celebrating family—
especially my mother, who took care of everyone—is so important to us. My mother was my everything. I always used to
tell her, "If anything happens to you, I'm going with you," and
she used to say to me, "Don't talk like that. Life goes on: you
have your kids; you've got to move on."

When I was growing up, my mom was always strict with
us. My father was, too, but he let us have whatever we wanted.
Then I got married and was wrapped up in my life with Joe. I
was also working in the fashion industry in New York City as a
buyer at Macy's and then a sales rep for Nine West and Calvin
Klein handbags, which consumed a lot of my time. The days
just flew by. The only opportunity I really got to be with my
mom was at our Sunday dinners. You don't appreciate your
mother as much during those stages in your life, because you're
so busy and it never crosses your mind that one day she won't
be there anymore. After that, I had Gia, stopped working, and

then had the other three girls. That's when my mom was around all the time, and that's when we became really, really close. I would call her ten to twenty times a day. I told her everything. She was my best friend. Even though she would still yell at me over little things, I knew it was because she wanted the best for me and her granddaughters. It tears me up inside that she's not here anymore. I feel like just when I started being able to really enjoy our relationship, she was taken away from me.

On the weekends when we had nothing going on I would always ask my parents, "What are you guys doing? Come over, come over." We used to do that with my brother a lot, too. Now, his kids have a lot of activities, like wrestling and stuff, but when their kids were younger, we were always together.

There's no doubt in my mind that my mom made me the mother I am today, even though we're opposites in many ways. My mom always enjoyed the simple and small pleasures in life. She never cared about what she looked like or what people thought of her, despite the fact that she always looked beautiful and everyone adored her. She taught me how to cook. She taught me everything, really—most important, she taught me how to be the best mom I could be to my daughters.

I posted an older picture on Instagram of my mom and me from Mother's Day 2015; it was of us together in Atlantic City. I'd taken her to a work event because she loved to go to the casino! The slots were her favorite. I remember we went out to dinner beforehand, and she was watching me take pictures with fans. We had so much fun! She was always so proud of me, as I was of her.

The only difficult thing about Mother's Day was not having Joe there. He did send me a beautiful arrangement of mixed flowers with hydrangeas, which I loved. That felt good, because I'd been doing double duty as Mom and Dad since he left, and I thought I deserved to be appreciated by him. I knew there was nothing I could do about the fact that he couldn't be with me in person, so I just made the best of it. I never want my girls to see me upset, so I try to keep my chin up and a smile on my face at all times, which isn't easy.

A week or so after that came my forty-fourth birthday. It was also a few weeks after filming had wrapped on season seven of *Real Housewives*, and I was asked to do a commercial for the movie *Independence Day: Resurgence*, starring Jeff Goldblum, Liam Hemsworth, and Bill Pullman, which was coming out July Fourth weekend.

When I first agreed to do the shoot, I didn't realize that it was scheduled for May 18. Since I'd spent my forty-third birthday in Danbury, I wanted to do something special. Taping a commercial wasn't exactly what I had in mind.

My good friend Lisa Fortunato was kind enough to let us use her amazing backyard for the summer-themed shoot, which would take place by her pool and a really cool tiki-type bar that was set up to make it look like a Fourth of July barbecue. They wanted to film at a gorgeous house with a pool that was close by. Lisa is one of my best friends, so she offered. She's amazing. I love her. She's always been there for me.

When I arrived at Lisa's house the crew was setting up for the shoot, but I just wasn't myself. My longtime makeup artist and good friend, Priscilla DiStasio, could tell that something wasn't right and asked me if I was okay. I told her that I was in a funk, but I didn't really tell her why.

To be honest, I didn't really know why. Maybe because I wasn't with my daughters. Or maybe because, as an adult, I've never loved celebrating my own birthday.

Priscilla, with her thick, unmistakable New York accent, told me in a joking tone, "Well, bitch, you better snap out of it, we've got work to do," as she playfully led me into her makeup chair. That made me crack a little smile.

As Priscilla started to work her magic, my lawyer, Jim, came in and said, "Melissa will be here in ten minutes."

Melissa? As in my sister-in-law Melissa?

Oh, *Madonna mia*! So much for my relaxing birthday. Not only did I have to work, but now I had to work with my sister-in-law. Ugh. It's not that I don't love Melissa; it's just easier to get along when we're not working together. At least when I was in Danbury the girls threw me a birthday party and I got to pamper myself at the makeshift spa with a massage from an inmate who happened to be a certified masseuse.

Jim could tell by my face that I was annoyed, and he looked at me and said, "Please don't start any trouble with her today.

Everything has been great with you two and we are going to keep it that way, capiche?"

I answered him back, "Whatever." That was exactly how I felt.

And he said, " 'Whatever'? What are you, a seventh grader? We're going to play nice, capiche?"

I rolled my eyes and said, "Fine, capiche."

He was right as usual.

Just a few weeks earlier, Melissa and I had done a photo shoot together for the "Hot Bodies" issue of *US Weekly*, where we dressed up like the lifeguards on Baywatch and I got to re-create an iconic Raquel Welch picture. The truth is we had a lot of fun together.

No sooner was Jim out of the room when in comes Melissa with her hair and makeup glam squad team, who I know from other *Housewives* shoots. They were all in such a great mood, so friendly and cheery, that it put me in an even worse mood, because I was absolutely miserable.

I can't explain it.

Melissa and I were making small talk about the kids and some *Housewives* gossip when the producers of the commercial came in to make sure we were comfortable with our lines. About twenty minutes later, Melissa and I went into the backyard and started filming the commercial. It took a few hours, but we finally got it done.

To be honest, I couldn't wait to leave so I could go home and go to bed. Even though it was my birthday, I was a little bit depressed, and I was sad because no one at the shoot even acknowledged that it was a special day for me.

Seriously? WTF?

Once the commercial wrapped, around four or five o'clock, I went inside Lisa's house to get my bag and I noticed that my brother, Joey, was there. I figured he was there to pick up Melissa. Surely *he* would remember my birthday.

Nothing. Nada. Zilch.

Next thing I knew, I looked up and saw my daughter Milania.

I wondered what she was doing there.

Then I saw Gia, Gabriella, Audriana; and Joey and Melissa's kids, Antonia, Gino, and Joey.

Next I saw my mother, and that's when I got teary-eyed.

It was an impromptu surprise party! No one had forgotten my birthday after all. Lisa had ordered some amazing dishes from one of my favorite places. The other Lisa, my dear friend Lisa Giammarino, had driven down from New York. Jim and Priscilla both stayed, and we all ate and drank and had a nice party.

I was finally in the mood to celebrate!

Right after we had cake—white with pink flowers—Joe called to wish me a happy birthday. He also had a card and red roses delivered to the house. Even though you can't send stuff yourself from prison, he was able to have someone on the outside do it for him, just as he did with my Mother's Day flowers.

We spent the rest of the night there, just hanging out. We

took a lot of pictures and I posted them on Instagram, because it felt really nice to be celebrated and just relax with friends and family surrounding me. Gia also posted one of the two of us with the caption, *Wishing my mom the happiest birthday and hoping all her wishes come true! Love you so much!*

I went to bed that night with a smile on my face; the only down side to the day was that I was one year older and Joe wasn't there with me.

I definitely didn't feel like I was forty-four. I felt more like I was in my mid- to late thirties. I don't want to be in my twenties anymore, but I still think I look and act younger than my age. I know it's a cliché, but I really do believe that age is just a number. It's all about how you feel and how you look. I have a lot of energy, and I take care of myself. I work out. I eat well. And I try to keep my stress level low, even though that's not easy as a single, working mom with four daughters!

Four days later, on Joe's birthday—which fell on a Sunday—the girls and I went to visit him in prison. We weren't allowed to bring him anything, but I sent him a birthday card so he knew that I was thinking of him. One of the things that got me through my eleven and a half months there was receiving notes and letters from people, whether it was friends, family, or fans. That way you have something you can read when you're bored. There's a lot of downtime.

I always try to bring the kids when I go see Joe because he misses them so much, but it's not always simple, because they have a lot of activities on the weekends. And since it's two hours away, we can't go during the week. They also go with Joe's mom when they can.

When visiting Joe in prison, there are always a lot of mixed emotions for me and my girls. Of course, we feel happiness because we're with him. But there's always a great deal of sadness because we know he has to be in there for so much longer and can't come home with us. Obviously, on days like his birthday, it makes it that much more of a challenge. I do feel sorry for him. And I do spend time thinking about what he's doing in there at any given moment on any given day, because I was in there, too, but—at the same time—I think, *Ugh, I can't believe my life is like this. Why didn't he do the right thing?* I'm a hard-ass that way. If he'd done the right thing, then this wouldn't be our life. It was nothing that I did. I didn't force him to do what he did. It was different for him when I went because he was living with a lot of guilt. He blamed himself, which he should have. Whereas I'm just angry that I'm doing everything by myself. I didn't sign up for this. I didn't sign up to have four kids without a father. As more time passes, I get more and more upset about it.

But, again, I just tell myself I have to push through it and focus on the positive—like a charity event I did in Atlantic City on June 2, 2016, to benefit Gilda's Club South Jersey. It was their sixth-annual "Cocktails by the Beach" fund-raiser, overlooking the Atlantic Ocean with 100 percent of ticket sales going to Gilda's Club, which is such an amazing charity. My lawyer, Jim, and his wife, Rebecca, were cochairing the event, because Jim's brother's wife, Karen, a young mother of two little girls, recently was diagnosed with breast cancer and thank God she survived. That's what got them involved in the charity, and when Jim asked me to help out, I of course said yes.

That night, I got to spend time with and help support men, women, and kids who either had cancer themselves or had a loved one with cancer. I signed copies of *Turning the Tables* and took a lot of photos with fans. The people I met really touched me with their stories. When the event was over, I started crying as Jim walked me out to the car that was waiting to drive me home. He asked me what was wrong, and I told him that being a part of the special evening had really moved me.

What was even more meaningful is that survivors kept saying to me, "You inspire me." I was thinking, *I inspire you? Wow.* I said, "No, *you* inspire me." The whole time I was there I couldn't help but realize that—compared to what these people had to go through—prison was nothing. As long as I have my health, I can get through anything. Everyone has horrible things they have to go through—different crosses to bear—but fighting for your life is on another level. They were all so strong, and I really admire that. It made me extra thankful for everything I do have, even though I've had a lot thrown at me and—some days—it feels overwhelming.

I pray for anyone who has to endure a terrible illness or disease. Or anything that's a major life obstacle. I try to go to church as often as possible, but even when I can't, I still pray all the time.

You have to. I truly believe that God only gives us what we can handle. I'm just hoping that I've had my share of that for a long time to come.

4

THE *PRESSURE* IS ON

*I*n June 2016, we started doing press for season seven of *Real Housewives of New Jersey*, which is usually a fun time. When the show first started, we used to travel more and go out to Los Angeles, but this time we pretty much stayed in the New York area, partly because I hadn't been home for that long and I wanted to be there for my girls as much as possible.

Another reason was that because I was still on supervised release, a form of probation, my travel was somewhat restricted. Jim had to get permission for me anytime I wanted to travel outside of New York or New Jersey. I wasn't thrilled about that, but there was nothing I could do.

I know some people get anxious about being interviewed on television, but I'm used to it by now. In the beginning, I always felt like Andy Cohen asked me the hardest questions when I did *Watch What Happens Live*. I didn't get it. I thought he hated me. I would say to Joe, "Why doesn't he like me?" But now I realize that he was just doing his job, and I was taking it personally, which I shouldn't have. I can tell he cares for me, too, because he reached out to me before I went to prison and while I was gone; we emailed each other very often. He kept my spirits up and kept me in the *Housewives* loop. He's a really great guy. If he were straight, I would definitely make out with him! And he's so funny and quirky.

In one way, doing press for the show is a major ego boost. So many people come up to me and say, "We love you, Teresa!" and a lot of fans tell me that I've inspired them with my strength, which feels really good. But all that attention can also be tricky, especially when I'm with my kids, and even more specifically, when my kids were younger. I remember I'd be trying to pay attention to them and make sure they didn't run off, while at the same time I never wanted to be rude to someone who recognized me and wanted to make a connection. I rarely ever say no to an autograph or a photo request, because they're my fans and they're putting themselves out there and supporting me. I always try to be as nice as I can be.

Although, sometimes, you do just want your privacy. There are times when I'm out with my friends and people are continually interrupting us, which makes me feel bad. But I know that's the price I pay for exposing my life on television. In New Jersey it's not as bad because people are used to me here. So, for example, when I'm in the supermarket or at my kids' schools or activities, I'm generally left alone.

However, when I leave the immediate area, it's a different story. When I took my family on a vacation to Puerto Rico in April, there were a lot of people who came up to me in the airport and while we were there. I took tons of photos. There was actually one fan who found out where we were staying and came to the hotel. He literally waited in the lobby every day until he ran into me. The nice thing was that he worked for Nutella—the company that makes that chocolate-and-hazelnut spread—and he brought me a backpack and lots of treats for my kids. He also gave me a really sweet card that read, "I was going through a rough time and you helped me get through it. I think you're so strong and amazing. You inspired me so much."

If you can believe it, the paparazzi also followed me to Puerto Rico. We'd just returned from a day of zip-lining, and all of the sudden I look up to see this guy taking my picture. I just smiled, even though I was shocked. It's easier when I'm prepared for it, like when I'm working.

Anyway, back to the press tour. It was me and Melissa doing appearances together, and Jacqueline, Siggy, and Dolores were doing other interviews separately. They'd do some shows and we'd do others. It was fun! Except for the interview I did with *Access Hollywood*, when I ended up walking off the set, because they asked me about Joe being deported. Believe me, I don't enjoy having to constantly be on the defensive, which is exactly what happened. It's not something I want my family to see or experience, especially my children. I was humiliated and pissed off by some of the questions. Melissa was humiliated and pissed off on my behalf as well. It's just not the way you treat someone, and I don't think I deserved it. Can you blame me for feeling like I need to protect myself and my kids from this kind of thing? I'd prefer for it not to be that way, but it is what it is.

And circumstances like this only make it more difficult for me and my girls to move on with our lives.

5

SUMMER LOVIN'

By the time summer 2016 came, I was so happy to be done with filming. Summer is my absolute favorite time of the year. I think because it reminds me of my childhood and, in particular, a very special trip I took to Italy with my parents when I was twelve years old and my brother, Joey, was ten. I'll never forget it—we were there for an entire month, which felt so glamorous and sophisticated. While I was exploring Europe, most of my friends were just going down to the Jersey Shore or hanging out at home.

I'd always believed that it was a very unique part of my heritage to have family in another country, especially when that country was Europe. I never grew up having grandparents around, like my daughters did and still do. We went to visit my dad's mom and got to learn so much about our history and our background. The last time I'd been to Italy was when I was two, right after my dad's father had passed away, so of course I didn't have any memory of that or appreciation for what that had been like.

To go back ten years later was a really big deal. I got to see where my parents were born—they're originally from Sala Consilina. It's a town in the province of Salerno, which is in the Campania area of southwestern Italy. It's only got 12,258 people living there, and it's still the most populated town of Vallo di Diano.

We actually returned there during season two of *Real Housewives*. Joe was born there and lived there for more than a year. My mom was pregnant with me when she came to the United States. She didn't speak any English at all. She said she would cry herself to sleep at night, stressing over why she'd ever left Italy and her family in the first place. Part of her wanted to go back, but she knew America was the land of opportunity, so she stayed.

You have to realize that my mom's mom died when she was ten, and her dad had left them right after she was born. He said he was going to go work in Venezuela and then he never came back. Can you imagine? I mean, it's hard enough without Joe, and he's only gone for three years! Her mother must have been a very strong woman. After her mother died, my mother was an orphan, so she was raised by her maternal grandmother.

I've always wanted to find my mother's father, but she never wanted to. We heard that he'd gotten remarried after moving to Venezuela, so my mother probably has half brothers and/or half sisters, who would be my aunts and uncles. When I started appearing on television and writing books, I thought they might see me and reach out, but they haven't. I'm sure my grandfather is dead, because he'd be in his late nineties by now, but if any of my mother's brothers, sisters, nieces, or nephews are reading this, I hope you do get in touch! I'd love to connect with you and get to know you.

Listen, I don't like what my grandfather did to my grandmother and mother, but I wouldn't let that stop me from meeting his other kids and their kids. Family is the most important thing. And since my mom never knew her father, I'd love to learn more about the man he was. Maybe we share some characteristics. Who knows?

I also have a lot of family in Belgium. That's where my paternal grandmother moved after my father's dad passed away. I have an uncle and an aunt who live there, and they both have five kids each. My uncle went to Belgium to go find work when he was in his twenties, and then met a girl, got married, and stayed there. Then his sister went to go visit him and she met a guy. She ended up getting married and staying there, too.

Anyway, back to my childhood Italy trip. You're not going to believe what happened while I was there! My husband, Joe—who obviously was not my husband at the time, but we already knew each other—was there, too. How crazy is that? He was also there on summer vacation with his family. We saw

each other while we were there and really liked each other—
we always really liked each other. I thought he was cute and
he was totally into me. Only I ended up meeting two other
guys—I kissed both of them, which was huge. At the time, I
was a complete prude, more so than all my friends.

If you can believe it, Joe ended up physically fighting with
one of the guys over me. We weren't even dating! It was just
a crush! Regardless, I'd started seeing this older guy—which,
in retrospect, was crazy because I was very young! It was just
while we were there for the month, and he came to my mom's
aunt's house, where we were staying. He was seventeen or
eighteen years old and able to drive there on his Vespa, which
I thought was so cool. I remember my mom just saying, "Oh
my God!" (If only she'd known the other guy I met was in
his twenties.) He ended up writing a letter to Joe and giving it
to my mother to send to Joe's aunt, saying that he wanted to
marry me! I swear to God. I couldn't make this shit up even if I
wanted to. I was twelve years old and my mother said, "You are
too young for any of this!" Now, thinking about the fact that
Gabriella is twelve, I can't believe it. *Madonna mia!*

But this guy, whose name I don't even remember, wanted
to let Joe know that he was staking his claim. That's what they
did back then.

Obviously it didn't work out, and Joe was the one who won
my heart after all. I never did talk to either of those guys again.
I wonder where they are today! It's so funny to think back on
that. It reminds me of how much Joe and I always loved each

other, even when we were way too young to be thinking about our future together.

What I also loved about that trip was the amazing meals we cooked and ate. The food was so fresh there, and everything tasted so delicious. Real, authentic Italian food isn't like the kind you find in American restaurants, which has a ton of artificial ingredients in it and thick, starchy sauces. We ate homemade pasta, cheese, and sausage. I remember thinking how different it was than what my friends thought of as Italian cuisine. I mean, I grew up eating that kind of stuff at home so, to me, it was second nature (even though it was better in Italy!), but people here don't get that. That's why my kids and I love food so much.

We went to the beach as well. They're so beautiful, even though they're made of stones rather than sand. It was an incredible experience, especially because all the people went topless with their barely there Brazilian bottoms. Even the little girls raced around with just bikini bottoms, which was so cute. I kept my top on, as did the rest of my family! I said, "There's no way I'm showing anyone my boobies!"

When we got home, I told my friends all about it and they couldn't believe everything I'd done. They just said, "Wow, you went to Italy for a month?" They were very impressed. I'll never, ever forget that trip. I'm planning to return next summer with my kids. Now that they're older, I really want them to appreciate where their *nonna*, *nonno*, and their father lived. And they want to go so badly. My father's brother still lives there, and my dad also has a lot of cousins there. Many of my mother aunts, uncles, and cousins are there, too. Tradition is so important to us.

That's why this past summer, once filming wrapped, I was so overjoyed to have the chance to relax and spend time at the Jersey Shore with my kids, like we've done many years past. It was no Italian getaway, but that didn't matter. We used to have a house there before we had to let it go—when we fell behind on the mortgage payments and after the home was damaged badly during Hurricane Sandy, so it was a place that I associated with tons of memories, some positive, some not so positive.

A lot of my friends have houses at the Shore, so we visited them some weekends. We spent Father's Day at Joey and Melissa's house down there with my kids and my parents. We just chilled out, barbecued, and swam in their pool. Everyone got along really well. My girls are very close with Joey and Melissa's sons and daughter. Then we decided to rent our own place on Long Beach Island for the month of August. It was nice and big and really gorgeous. It was just me and my daughters, and then my parents came one weekend. Sadly, we only used it for about two weeks, going back and forth, because there was so much else going on at home. I also became a member of the lake in our town, so we spent a lot of time there.

It was the first summer in a long time that I felt like I could really unwind. We went to the beach. We went out to eat. It was easy. I used to love to lie out and tan, but I don't do that anymore. Now I'm more conservative with the sun. I wear a hat and bring a chair and umbrella. I don't want wrinkles!

Joe doesn't love the beach the way I do—in years past, I would bring all the stuff and he'd end up meeting us there, but not staying the whole time—although I'm sure when he gets out of prison, he'll have a different perspective!

Of course I missed being there with Joe; it would have been great for him to be with us.

Unfortunately, I just had to rely on the memories.

6

BACK IN THE SWING OF THINGS

*W*hen September rolled around, it was just about time for the kids to go back to school. My feelings are always mixed about this. I love, love, love summer, so I hate saying goodbye to it. In the same vein, after spending more than two months straight with all four girls every day—and no husband to help out!—that year I was definitely ready for them to return to their regular schedule. My children have never gone to camp, because we had a house at the Shore, so we were together non-stop. I'm always thinking of new activities for us to do, like going to the lake or boating. I try to appreciate every minute with them, because things get so busy during the school year. It's bittersweet for me when summer comes to an end, because I'm running around like a madwoman shopping with each of my daughters individually at the Mall at Short Hills or any other boutiques, like Kids At Heart in Livingston. Obviously, that's fun for the girls and me. Who doesn't love to shop?! When Gia was a toddler we used to go to the mall almost every day, often as an indoor activity if it wasn't nice out. Unfortunately, these days we're in more of a rush. We have to get all of their supplies, too. It's a total shit show multiplied by four!

But before they went back, we took one last weekend on Long Beach Island at the Jersey Shore with my parents. It was so relaxing. We went to the beach and out to dinner. My parents have never been able to get enough of the beach, especially my mom. I must have inherited that from her! When I was growing up, we used to go to the Shore every Sunday and Wednesday—to Sandy Hook and Long Branch. Those were the days my father was off from work, so we would take day trips.

I remember my parents would make these delicious lunches, with big Italian sandwiches—like prosciutto with cheese, or chicken cutlets—for us to take to the beach. Everything tastes better with the sand between your toes! I have such vivid memories of being hot and hungry and so grateful for my parents' yummy food!

That trip reminded me of those days, when I had no worries. No stress. All I had to do was enjoy life. That's why on September 1, when summer was wrapping up, I posted a selection from a poem called "Hold Fast To Your Dreams," by Louise Driscoll on Instagram:

Hold fast your dreams!
Within your heart
Keep one still, secret spot
Where dreams may go,
And, sheltered so,
May thrive and grow
Where doubt and fear are not.
O keep a place apart,
Within your heart,
For little dreams to go!

I would say I've always been a dreamer, which is why the poem inspired me. All my life, I've tried to envision what I want to happen. And every time I've wanted something really badly I've gotten it. The thing is, now that I'm older, I'm scared. I have more responsibility. I have four mouths to feed and no one to help me do that, at least not for the time being. I don't have the luxury of just sitting back and fantasizing. What I do need to be doing, though, is envisioning what the rest of my career looks like. What if *Housewives* goes away? What's my next step? I don't want to stop working. I *can't* stop working, so I get worried.

I think this poem reminded me of who I used to be. And it alerted me to the fact that I still have that dreamer inside me, despite the reality that I carry the burden of keeping my family afloat financially and have for many years. I'm a very passionate person by nature, and I do want to build an empire. I'd love to do a swimwear line, bags, shoes, and activewear. I love fashion, and since it's also my background, I want to keep the momentum going.

It's like there are two sides of me—my mom side and my professional side. And since I'd spent the summer focusing on the former, I was ready to amp up the latter. I hate being bored, and I was concerned that with the kids heading back to school and the show not filming that I was going to get antsy. I'm not someone who can sit still and do nothing all day. Even if I'm home alone, I'm always cleaning, organizing, or working out.

My friend Lisa F. had one final summer party at her parents' home a couple of days before school started and we all switched gears. It was amazing and a great way to cap off the season. Gia and Milania were there, as were Siggy and a few other friends. The house is insanely gorgeous. It has this huge, elaborate fountain, which we all took a picture in front of. I felt really pretty that day in my pink dress and pink-and-orange hat. Too bad Joe wasn't around to appreciate it!

Two days later, the new school year kicked off and things returned to our normal, crazy schedule. Gia is big into competitive cheerleading. Gabriella does soccer on a club team. Milania is into soccer, basketball, and track. She likes to try a little bit of everything. And Audriana does gymnastics and competitive dance—ballet, jazz, and tap. She does back-walkovers in the living room! So of course I'm the one who has to sign them up for all that stuff and pay for it. And, let me tell you, it's not cheap.

I don't care, though. That's why I work so hard. I want to give my children the benefit of everything. When I was younger, I didn't do activities. I came home from school, did my homework, and then we had family dinner. It's different now. This is what kids these days do. They see what their friends are doing and what they have and they want the same thing. It's not always easy keeping up with the Joneses. But I try. And I do it all by myself. When I was away, I wasn't able to be around for my family or provide for them in the way I'm accustomed to.

This is why, when Audriana's seventh birthday arrived on September 14, I wanted to do something really special for her. So, at Audriana's request, I took her; her best friend, Olivia; Olivia's mom; and my friend Lisa G. to American Girl in New York City. It's all the rage with her and her peers, and they did a small private event for us, which was so fabulous. You have lunch there and bring your American Girl doll. It wasn't a big blowout bash, but it was exactly what Audriana wanted, and that made both of us very happy.

Of course, when it came to Gabriella's twelfth birthday, in October, she asked for a big party at our house. I wanted to give that to her, because I'd been in prison for her birthday the year before, which she'd said was one of her best birthdays, despite my not being there. While I was very glad to hear that, I also knew from Joe that she'd really missed me that day, which made me feel so sad. That's why I wanted to do something even better for her now that I was home.

We had the party at our house, in the backyard, for about forty kids. I got a DJ. I rented a mechanical bull and this inflatable ride called the Meltdown, which is basically straight out of that show *Wipeout* on ABC, where people have to jump over and duck under these moving arms. It was so fun! I also got Gabriella's name spelled out in these huge balloons and filled up our game room in all blue and silver balloons, the whole ceiling was covered, even though the festivities were mainly outside.

I always serve a lot of food, because I love to cook, eat, and play hostess. We had a bunch of varieties of pizza—macaroni, chicken Parmesan, eggplant, sausage and peppers. I think I ordered every single kind available. And I had an elaborate candy table. But the pièce de résistance for sure was Gabriella's cake, which was a gigantic light blue number twelve with edible sparkles all over it. Actually, each number was its own cake on these big silver bases that read, "Happy Birthday" on one side and "Gabriella" on the other. It was beyond gorgeous and delicious!

I definitely felt like I made up for not being there when she turned eleven. She said it was her best birthday by far, even better than the year before. Sure, she was sad that, this time, it was Joe who couldn't be there, but she was also so happy to get to tell her father about it when he called later in the day. She said, "Daddy, my party was amazing! Everyone had so much fun!" Joe holds a very special place in her heart, in all the girls' hearts. That's one of the reasons why I'm so pissed that he made such a mess of everything.

Later that month was my mom's sixty-sixth birthday, which—like Mother's Day—I had no idea would be the last one I ever spent with her. It's heartbreaking just to think about that. I am glad, though, that we had such a nice celebration for her at Joey and Melissa's house. We all had dinner together—me and my kids, my mom, my dad, Joey, Melissa, and their kids. My parents cooked together, even though it was my mom's special day. They love to be in control of the cooking! Melissa actually learned her way around a kitchen from my mother. Joey doesn't cook much, but he loves food and recently opened up a restaurant in New Jersey. I guess you don't have to be a chef to be a restaurateur.

We took some really beautiful photos that day, which I cherish. There's one of my mother with all seven of her grandchildren, sitting in front of her cake, which read, "Happy Birthday Nonna." It was white icing with red roses. She was so joyous that day. We all were. The only thing I was unhappy about was my hair! I had to wear a hat because I didn't like how it looked. Aside from that, we all had dinner together, hung out, and just enjoyed one another's company.

The best part was when I gave her the gift I'd gotten her— a trip to Punta Cana in the Dominican Republic. It was actually for my mom and dad, for both their birthdays. It was a total surprise. They hadn't been away together in a long time, since she hadn't been feeling great due to her rheumatoid arthritis, and I just wanted them to have a luxurious trip alone. They'd never splurge on something like that for themselves. It made me feel so proud to be able to do that for them, and they were very grateful. They ended up going in November and, when they came back, I took lots of pictures of them because they looked so tan and gorgeous!

Of course my mother's birthday celebration was also a nice distraction for me, because that same day—October 23—was my seventeen-year wedding anniversary to Joe. He had two gorgeous bouquets of flowers sent to me. One was a mixed bouquet with a card that read, "Happy Anniversary. Love you with all my heart, Joe." And the other was an enormous arrangement of two-dozen red roses.

It was really nice of him. I'm guessing he had his brother or his uncle or one of his friends send them to me. But it definitely didn't alleviate the sting of his not being there in person.

It wasn't easy with him gone. It's still difficult. And milestones tend to shine a bright light on that. The only thing I could do was try to keep myself going and not dwell on it. That's why when the kids went back to school and we were no longer filming the show, I started doing a lot of yoga again. It's much tougher to find the time for it when I have a busy work schedule. I like going to classes when I can, rather than doing it at home, because I prefer to be around people. It motivates me. Also, when my kids are in school and I have off from the show, sometimes I get bored. And when I'm bored I start to think about stuff, like Joe being away, and financial concerns, which makes me feel depressed and unlike my typically energetic self. Yoga helps center me.

If you think I'm lying about being more centered, guess who I reunited with and did yoga with around this time?

Danielle Staub.

That's right. My long-lost nemesis from seasons one and two. The one I famously flipped the table on and called a "prostitution whore."

I hadn't seen or spoken to Danielle in years, but some people on social media were telling me that she was saying nice things about me and it seemed like she had made a lot of changes in her life like I did. And I learned that she was into yoga.

The next thing I knew we had a date set—first yoga—then a casual lunch to catch up on lost time.

We snapped a picture together of us doing a yoga pose side by side and the *Housewives* universe went nuts.

She and I both laughed about it, but to be honest it was nice to reconnect with her.

Yoga can be a tremendous healer.

I wish I could do it all the time! But even when I'm not actively into *Housewives*, I'm still promoting myself and the show. For example, I went on *The Dr. Oz Show* in October, too. It was my first time sitting down with him and he was so kind. Just a really nice guy. I was very excited about that, even though I do get nervous whenever I go on talk shows.

I had butterflies when I spoke to Dr. Oz—I find radio much

easier than television in front of an audience—but I had a sense of what he was going to ask me and he stuck to it. He didn't bring up anything that crossed a line about Joe being deported. He did, however, very nicely inquire how Joe was doing and how I was doing, without getting snarky, which was appropriate.

I was very thankful for that, because—like I said—I'm sick of people trying to take me down.

I'm *so* done with that.

7

THE DONALD FOR PRESIDENT

I've never been particularly interested in politics. The latest in fashion, yes. The latest in what's happening in Hollywood, I'm all in. But Washington, eh, it's never really been my thing.

Until 2016.

With Donald Trump running for president, my interest was piqued.

Let me start off by saying that when I had the privilege of being on *The Celebrity Apprentice*, in 2011, all my experiences with Mr. Trump and everyone from the Trump organization were nothing but amazing and very professional. They made me feel extremely comfortable, because when I was first asked to join the cast of *The Celebrity Apprentice*, I wasn't sure if I should say yes. I'd heard mixed things about it, and my kids

were still young. I didn't want to be away from them for a
long period of time. But the show really wanted me, so they
called me and said, "Why don't you come in and meet with
Mr. Trump himself? And then you can decide if it sounds like
something you'd be interested in." They told me the names of
some of the other celebrities who'd already committed, but I
still wasn't 100 percent sure I'd fit in. So I took them up on the
opportunity to speak to Mr. Trump in person. Why not?

They invited both Joe and me to his office in Manhattan's
Trump Tower. I found out he lives in the same building—in
the penthouse! I remember wanting to look very professional
that day, so I wore a conservative suit and, even though Joe
didn't wear a suit and tie, I made sure he looked really nice.

When we arrived Mr. Trump was so welcoming. He and
Joe hit it off immediately. It was like they'd been friends for
years. I couldn't believe how gorgeous the office was. Not only
was it huge, but it had ridiculous views of New York City, including Central Park. There was stuff everywhere. He's definitely a knickknack person, which I can relate to! The walls
were lined with framed awards—like one of the Tree of Life
he received from the Jewish National Fund, which he's very
proud of. There were also a number of photographs; one of
him with Ronald Reagan, and another with John F. Kennedy
Jr. And there were tons of magazines framed—*Newsweek*, *GQ*,
Fortune, and so many more. He's one of the few men to have
been on the cover of *Playboy*. I couldn't believe it when I saw
that!

Then he had a whole table of sports memorabilia, like Mike Tyson's boxing belt and Shaquille O'Neal's basketball sneaker, which was enormous! Apparently Shaq took it off after one of his games and handed it to him. How cool is that?

I'd love to have an empire and an office like his one day.

The thing that surprised me the most, though—even more than the *Playboy* cover—was how incredibly nice he was. He said he really wanted me to be on the show. I told him my issue was that I wouldn't be able to see my kids for over a month while we were taping—if I made it through to the end. So he said they'd make an exception since I had four young children. In addition to the suites they provided for me and all the other cast members, they got me a second suite next door so that Joe and the girls could come visit on the weekends. I guess they never do that, but I was extremely grateful that he understood my predicament. Mr. Trump has five children of his own. He's a family man, so he got it. And my kids had the best time spending weekends in the city with me, because I did end up staying for the entirety of the filming process. Even after I got "fired" in task thirteen, I was on Arsenio Hall's team for the finale.

Honestly, I wasn't shocked that I made it that far. I know people make fun of me because I'm not always the most articulate person, but that doesn't mean I'm not smart. I know what's going on, believe me. Sure, I was nervous at first. Who wouldn't be? It's the same with anything that's brand-new. You're excited. You're not sure what to expect. And, you know, people will come at you, because they really want to win.

But I'm kind of a daredevil. And, back then, I wasn't afraid of anything. I'm still not.

Plus, I knew there were going to be some other cast members who'd be fun to hang out with. Victoria Gotti ended up becoming a close friend. She's great, and, despite the fact that she left early, we really connected. We still keep in touch. In fact, I'd say everyone was really nice, except Penn Jillette. He wasn't the easiest to work with or be around. Aubrey O'Day used to flirt with him all the time, which I thought was gross. I just wanted to be professional and focus on raising money for my charity, the NephCure Foundation (now called NephCure Kidney International), an organization committed to funding research and finding a cure for debilitating kidney disease. I was project manager three times—tasks seven, nine, and thirteen. Even though I lost task seven, I wasn't eliminated. Then I won task nine and lost task thirteen, which is when I was "fired." The good news is that I raised seventy thousand dollars for NephCure, which is what the show is all about. That's another thing about Mr. Trump; he's very philanthropic, and so am I. I believe you have to give of yourself to those less fortunate than you are.

I also admire his unbelievable work ethic. Since he was always so busy with his other professional obligations, we only saw him when we were filming the boardroom scenes, which took hours upon hours, because they like to spice things up.

Still, the fact that someone I knew personally and held in

such high regard was running for president, had me super interested and glued to the television during election time. I found myself tuning away from Bravo (sorry, Andy Cohen!) and watching the programs on CNN or Fox News. I couldn't believe what I was seeing and hearing; it was way more dramatic than *Housewives*!

For a few months I really became hooked. It was unbelievable to observe how divided our country was when it came to Hillary Clinton and Donald Trump. And, especially, to listen to people saying so many negative things about Trump and his family.

I'd become close with Ivanka, as well as Don Jr., Eric, and his now wife, Lara, during my time on *Celebrity Apprentice*, so I was disturbed at what I was seeing on television about their family. It reminded me of what my own family went through, though, of course, the Giudice drama was on a much smaller scale. I know firsthand how cruel the media or the "fake media" can be, and I empathized.

I know he says things that may rub people the wrong way, but he's our president, and no matter what people's personal opinions of him are, I believe he deserves a certain level of the country's respect. People need to look at the facts before jumping to conclusions, especially because I don't even think he means to offend people. He just says what's on his mind and we live in a hypersensitive world. I know how that feels.

I remember in the days after I was released from prison, my

phone was ringing off the hook with people calling and texting, telling me that they were glad I was home and that they were thinking of me and my kids.

One of the very first calls I received was from Ivanka Trump. She also sent me a beautiful note. I was so flattered. She really is a class act.

I wanted to let her and her brothers know that I was there to back them up, too. I found myself communicating through email and via direct message on Twitter with the Trump children, offering them my support when I saw something particularly horrible. They responded every time and thanked me for reaching out with personal messages. They even asked me how my girls were doing. Again, so classy. It made me respect and root for them even more.

On the night of the election I watched all the live coverage, flipping back and forth between channels. I stayed up well past 2:00 a.m. I was so happy for Donald Trump and his children when he won, but I was also nervous because I knew how difficult the road ahead would be for our new president.

As I said, I've never been a political person. All I know about Hillary Clinton is what I saw on TV. When I watched CNN, she was the savior; when I watched Fox she was the devil. I rooted for Mr. Trump because I actually had the pleasure of getting to know him and his family. And I'd developed a tremendous amount of respect for each of them. It's not easy to be in the spotlight like that. Even though they were accustomed to it on some level, this was a whole new ball game.

If I'd ever had the fortune of meeting Hillary Clinton, who knows, maybe I would have agreed with the people on CNN. I will say I did like the idea of having a female president, just not one named Hillary Clinton. I think Bill Clinton messed things up for her, kind of like Joe did for me. Also, I don't understand why she didn't get in trouble for all those emails she sent. Why did I get in trouble and she didn't? It doesn't make any sense to me.

My only regret is that I couldn't vote for Mr. Trump because I was on probation from being in prison. Unfortunately, I wasn't allowed.

The last thing I'll say about politics is that Kimberly Guilfoyle, the cohost of *The Five* on Fox News Channel, is absolutely gorgeous. She has amazing hair and really knows her stuff. She could totally be a Housewife!

Andy Cohen, you should call her.

Speaking of which . . .

In addition to Election Day, November also brought with it the *Real Housewives* season seven reunion. Oh boy! The reunion shows always get very heated.

Of course Bravo kept us all apart until we were sitting on the couches onstage, so there was no opportunity for us to talk ahead of time, which was good.

I was sitting on one couch with Melissa. Jacqueline, Siggy, and Dolores were on the other couch. The only tension was between Jacqueline and me (even my yoga practice couldn't help with that!). And Jacqueline and Melissa. I thought Jacqueline was my friend, but she wasn't. I believe she actually plotted to destroy my life. She was the puppeteer, choreographing every scene so that people would think I was the bad guy.

I'd say that the reunion ended up being therapeutic for me and provided me with a sense of closure. I felt like I got certain points across. I was frustrated that Siggy and Dolores weren't asked more pointed questions about the situation between Jacqueline and me. It would have been nice if Andy had tried to get them to give more of their opinion. Unfortunately, that didn't happen. But, regardless, it felt like a relief just to let it all out. I kept thinking, *I need to release this before I can move on. Out with the old, in with the new.*

After the reunion, it was a welcome change to celebrate Thanksgiving at the end of the month with the people I love and cherish most. Even though it's been a tough couple of years for me, I'm still very grateful for all the blessings in my life and the family and friends who've supported me through the worst of times.

In the past we've spent Thanksgiving cooking and eating a big meal together with my parents, with Joey and Melissa's family, with Joe's side, or any combination of all three. It's always been a special holiday, because we come together as a group to enjoy one another's company and a delicious feast. It's not often that we can do that, because everyone typically has a million things going on in their lives—the kids with school and their activities, and the adults with their parenting duties and their work commitments.

This year, however, I wanted to start the day off with something different. With Joe gone, I wasn't in the cheeriest mood, and I didn't feel like dwelling on that. I decided to filter my sadness and frustration into doing charitable work, which has long been something that's very important to me, even before I went on *The Celebrity Apprentice*. I thought it would be nice to continue that tradition with my girls, so I said to them, "Since Daddy's not here with us this Thanksgiving, let's all spend the morning helping to feed those less fortunate than we are. People who may not have family or friends or even anything to eat for the holiday." And they all said yes! I was so happy that they were that enthusiastic about it. It was a proud mommy moment!

My friend told me about a place called Elijah's Promise in New Brunswick, New Jersey. They run a soup kitchen, culinary school, catering business, and a café. They serve more than one hundred thousand meals a year and train people to work in the food industry. When I heard that, I thought it was completely amazing and wanted to get involved in any way I could.

I also thought it was necessary for the girls to see that our lives are very privileged, which is not the norm. I wasn't sure how they would do with it once we got there, but I was thrilled by how they handled themselves. They put their whole hearts into it. Everybody was impressed with them, because they worked so hard and had a great time. They were super friendly, chatting away, setting the tables, serving plates of food. There's nothing better than being able to give back to your community, especially on such a meaningful day. It was truly the best!

After Elijah's Promise, we spent the afternoon with Joe's family. They cooked so much food! And I remember we did that mannequin challenge thing at the table, which was funny. We all had to freeze and then someone recorded it. It was a really nice time. Even though Joe's mom places some of the blame on me for what happened, she adores the girls, and manages to treat me kindly.

We definitely missed Joe—it's always harder on special occasions—but we did get to speak to him. He said, "Have a good time. I love you so much." Holidays are not the right time for visitation, because the inmates have their own stuff going on, which distracts them in a good way. The prisons serve much better food than on normal days. They try to make it as pleasant as possible for the inmates. Of course it's still sad, but when you're in there, you don't even think about that. Every day is just the same day.

I remember when I was in there, they would make this whole production of decorating for the holidays, and I would think to myself, *Do you need to really do that? It's not going to fool me into believing I'm not in prison.* You have to realize, though, that a lot of these people are in there for years and years, so that's their life. That's their family. That's who they're going to hang out with day in and day out. They have to pretend like that's their home. I wasn't in there for that long. It may seem strange to say, but I'm grateful that if I had to be incarcerated at all, it was only for a short amount of time.

The Sunday after Thanksgiving, we celebrated with my family, so it was me and the kids, Joey and Melissa and their kids, and my parents. We do turkey, ham, stuffing, mashed potatoes, pies—everything! The girls adore being with their cousins.

Overall we had a wonderful holiday. We tried something new and we upheld our ritual of surrounding ourselves with loved ones.

I was *almost* able to forget that my husband wasn't there. *Almost.*

That's the thing, even if I can't forget—even if it eats me up inside—I need to continue to move forward. I need to keep my head held high and carry on for myself and for my four daughters.

8

A VERY UNMERRY ·CHRISTMAS

*W*hen my mother first got sick, it came out of nowhere. She'd been struggling with her rheumatoid arthritis for a long time, but that wasn't going to kill her.

On December 6—I'll never forget that day—my father called me in a panic because my mother had passed out at home. Her blood pressure had dropped and he said, "Your mother just fell! You have to come over here right now." They lived about fifteen minutes away from me, so I jumped in the car and called an ambulance at the same time. I thought, if she's lying on the floor, I won't be able to pick her up and my father is too weak himself, so I'll need help.

The ambulance and I arrived at the same time. They took her to St. Joseph's hospital in Wayne, New Jersey, and my father and I followed closely behind. Immediately, they told us that she had pneumonia. I remember saying, "What do you mean pneumonia?! Where did this come from?" My dad said she'd had the chills and the runs the night before, but no fever or cold, thank God.

They kept her in the hospital for two days to make sure things were stable. Only then she started having trouble breathing, so they had to put her on a breathing tube. That was the hardest thing to watch; the tube was so big. For some reason it was the only size they had. The ones she was on later were much smaller and less traumatic-looking. Despite that, I have to say that all the doctors and nurses there were amazing. My brother and I never left her side. We were there every single day. We took turns sleeping in the chair that was next to her bed. The only time I snuck out for a little bit was to drive my kids to their activities. Fortunately, a lot of my kids' friends' parents helped me out, because I didn't even want to leave her for a minute. I would sleep there one or two nights, and then Joey would take over. My brother and I live in the same town, so he was close by as well. My dad was there all the time, too. He was heartbroken. It was so hard to watch him crying over my mother. Melissa came also, but she couldn't be there as often because someone had to be home with their three kids. And she had to run Envy, her clothing store. We were all a mess, but we were together as a family, just the way my mother wanted.

Still, at this point, it wasn't even a thought in our minds that she could die. My father had been on a breathing tube before and had come out fine. They'd told us she was very sick. But she made it through. My mom was so strong and resilient. Every day, I would ask the doctors, "When is she going to get off this tube?" We couldn't wait for that to happen. We would just be sitting there, watching her, all day. Amazingly, the hours and the minutes passed quickly, even though you'd think it would have been the reverse.

After five days, they finally took the tube out. Unfortunately, then she started having trouble breathing again and they had to put it back in that night. So she was on it for two more weeks. Then after that they had to take it out, because you're not supposed to be on it for more than that amount of time. That's also when they had to do a tracheotomy. To me, that was the most distressing thing ever. I didn't understand what a trach tube was. I thought she would have to talk holding a machine to her neck for the rest of her life. Fortunately, that was not the case. To tell you the truth, if I would have known what a tracheotomy was, I would have suggested they trach her from the beginning, because it's actually less traumatic for the patient and less traumatic than watching someone on a breathing machine every single day. It takes a toll on you. But I guess they don't do it that way.

Once they performed the tracheotomy, my mother started waking up. When she had the breathing tube, she was out, so all we did was watch her sleep. It was breathing for her, but they still kept her sedated, because imagine a tube down your throat! You would go nuts. So for about two and a half weeks we couldn't talk to her or communicate with her at all. My father had been on a breathing tube for only a day or two—this was all new and unsettling for us.

When my mom first passed out at her house, she fell on the right side of her body, which meant her whole right side wasn't working well. She was only moving her left side. We had to call a neurologist in to check her brain with CAT scans. She went through so much, because they didn't know if she'd had a stroke or what. After so many tests, they said she'd have to have surgery in the back of her neck, because there were these discs pressing against it and that would help her to move her right side again. We transferred her to St. Joseph's in Patterson. They did a cauterization to make sure her heart was strong enough to do the surgery—I found out later that she'd had a mini heart attack during that period. They did try to do the surgery, but they said one of her veins was 70 percent blocked and that her blood pressure dropped too low, so they had to stop. Eventually, she would need a stent. They told my brother afterward that she almost died. He didn't tell me or our dad that until much later. He was trying to protect both of us.

Around this time I had an opportunity to do a television show in Los Angeles with Milania that would have raised money for a charity of my choice. The charity I'd selected was Dina Manzo's Project Ladybug, an amazing organization that I'd done work for in the past.

Jim did all the paperwork, and our flights and hotel were

booked, but I had to cancel at the last minute. The thought of going to California with my mother lying in a hospital bed was just not something I was ready to do.

So with my mother in the hospital and no immediate signs of her being released, I realized that I was going to have to cancel our Christmas vacation. I was planning to take my friends, their families, my daughters, and my parents to Punta Cana. My kids hadn't been away in three years. When all our legal troubles arose, we weren't allowed to leave the country. Then I went to prison. And then Joe went to prison. They were really looking forward to it. We all were.

At first, since I thought my mom was on the mend, I just canceled my parents' reservations. I knew there was no way she'd be able to go even if she did feel better or get sent home from the hospital. I waited as long as I could to make that decision. I figured, okay, so she had pneumonia, but people recover from that.

I was hopeful for a while, thinking maybe she'd regain enough strength to make the trip. She'd never been hospitalized or even sick like that before. But after two weeks, around the time she went on the breathing tube, I knew it wasn't in the cards for her to go anywhere.

I still waited before withdrawing for the rest of us. I was so sure she was going to make it through and be fine. Although, once it became clear that she wasn't getting out of intensive care, there was no way I could leave with a clear conscience.

None of us would have been able to unwind or enjoy the vacation in the way we'd hoped to without the peace of mind of knowing that my mother was recovering.

We were supposed to leave on December 27, which was my parents' forty-seventh wedding anniversary. It was going to be their anniversary and Christmas gift from me. They'd had so much fun there in November that I figured we'd all go back to Punta Cana together. The Dominican Republic is really beautiful. And we all needed to feel the sun on our faces and chill out after a very long and challenging few years.

Unfortunately, that didn't happen. The kids understood and, of course, we all knew that their *nonna*'s health was the most important thing of all. Still, we were bummed out, to say the least, even though there was nothing we could do. I really didn't want to disappoint my kids. I knew that they had their hearts set on the trip and they really deserved it after everything they'd been through.

You have to understand that, even though I know that what happened to me wasn't my fault and that there was no criminal intent whatsoever, that didn't make it any easier for my kids. Which—again—is why when people call me a criminal, I wish they knew the truth. It's no day at the beach, believe me.

Recently, I was at a fashion show and there were these twentysomething girls who shouted the word "criminal" at me. And, I just thought, *Really? You don't know me. You don't know who I really am. You only know the version of me that you see on television. You think that's what I'm like all the time?* Listen,

I get that they were young and naive and that they have their whole lives ahead of them to learn how to act appropriately and treat others with respect, but still. They should figure out how to keep their mouths shut, because they don't know what's going to happen to them in their future. I used to run my mouth like that, too, and look what happened to me. I used to be very naive. I grew up in an extremely sheltered home.

But I digress . . .

Once our vacation and my trip to California were off the schedule, I turned my attention to Christmas festivities, which I was not at all into. I was just sad and depressed. Joe was away. My mom was in the hospital. Our vacation was a bust. And, what was even more upsetting was that Christmas has traditionally been one of my favorite times of year. Sure, it's always been a lot of work, too, with decorating, buying and wrapping the presents, and cooking, but I was happy to do all of it when things were good for our family. I wanted to create for my kids the same kind of amazing memories I had from my own childhood.

When I was growing up, Joey and I used to race downstairs early in the morning on the twenty-fifth to find lots of presents under the tree. Nothing extravagant—that wasn't the way we were raised—but we never wanted for anything. That was important to my father. He worked hard to provide for all of us. And, the thing is, it wasn't about the gifts. It was about celebrating with our loved ones. We used to have about thirty-five people over to our house on Christmas Eve. You know, the

Feast of the Seven Fishes—it's an Italian-American tradition. So we'd all cook together. Me, my mom, and my dad. We'd make different fish and seafood and then all sorts of desserts, like struffoli, which are these little Italian honey cakes in the shape of balls with sprinkles on them. They're super easy to make. It's just flour, eggs, honey, water, salt, butter, sprinkles, and a few other ingredients. Some people use a dash of wine, or lemon and orange zest. They're *delicioso!*

Preparing and eating all the food is my strongest memory of the holidays back then. Gifts were not the focus. It was about the people, the meal, and sitting around the table together.

Even after Joe and I got married and had kids we carried on those customs. We'd spend Christmas with his family and my family, sometimes both, which was really nice. We would make somebody dress up like Santa Claus every year, which the kids loved. And I'd be up into the middle of the night wrapping the presents. I mean, I know people have seen on *Real Housewives* that we used to do Christmas *big* before we had legal and financial troubles. I'm sure people judged us for the excess, but I don't care. At the time, Joe's businesses were very successful and we had the means to do it. I don't understand what's wrong with that. Our girls are good girls. They're not spoiled brats. They're grateful for everything they're given, so what's the problem with going all out once in a while?

Anyway, because I came home so close to Christmas in 2015—I was released from prison just two days before—we couldn't really, truly celebrate properly. We were all still recovering. So, I wanted this year to be special for my girls, despite the fact that I was really down and Joe was gone. Since we'd been planning to leave for vacation on December 27, and Joey and Melissa had been planning to leave on the twenty-sixth, we were going to re-create the same Feast of the Seven Fishes experience from our childhood at my brother's house with all our kids and my parents. But, with my mom in the hospital, we decided to do something much more low-key.

The girls and I still went to Joey and Melissa's house for Christmas Eve; only we didn't cook. My father was at the hospital; he wouldn't leave my mom's side. It was really just for the kids that we celebrated. We got dressed up. I wore a long black halter dress with a peephole front. Melissa wore a very pretty, shorter red dress, and she ordered in food for the group. She had another couple over and we basically had dinner, opened a few gifts, took some photos in front of the tree, which was stunning with its white lights and gold flowers and ribbon, and the kids played in the game room—that was it. We'd been to the hospital that day, too, so the mood wasn't as festive as it normally would have been.

On Christmas Day, we had our own tree and presents at home. I was at the hospital with my mom all day, and the kids went to visit their father's family. In the past few years, we haven't done things as over the top as we once did. You have to do what's right at the time. In 2015, Gia and Joe took on a lot of what I'd typically have done myself. And, even this past year, 2016, Gia was up with me late on Christmas Eve, helping wrap all the gifts. I remember her saying, "Wow, Mom, this is so much work. I can't believe it." I said, "I know! Christmas is draining!"

The one nice thing about being away for eleven and a half months—probably the only nice thing—is that everyone realizes how much you do for them on a day-to-day basis. My kids definitely did, and Joe did, too. That's why I always try to look at everything in a positive way. Maybe I needed to go away in order for Joe to appreciate me more.

That said, it wasn't the Christmas any of us had hoped for. Without my mom there, and especially with her in the hospital, I felt empty, sad, and unmotivated to celebrate.

What I didn't know was that we wouldn't have a truly joyous Christmas again for a long time to come.

9

A TURN FOR THE WORSE

*B*y the time the New Year rolled around, we couldn't wait to get my mom into the rehabilitation facility for patients who've had tracheotomies. Also, since she'd been lying in bed in the hospital for a month, her muscles were atrophying and she was very weak. On top of that, she already had rheumatoid arthritis. There was no way we could bring her home without a nurse to be with her 24-7. And there was no way my father would have been able to completely take care of her. Neither could I. I had four kids to deal with on my own. I couldn't believe it was yet another horrible thing for my family to deal with. *When would it end? Why was this happening to us?*

Still, even though I was beside myself, I was happy that the breathing tube was out. All I wanted was for her to be awake.

She wasn't able to communicate with us right away, because it takes time and practice to be able to talk and make sounds after a tracheotomy, but eventually she was able to speak to us. That was a relief.

The plan was for her to go to rehab, have the trach removed so the hole could close up, and then go back to her normal life. But things didn't go as smoothly as we would have liked. While she was in rehab, it was always something. Her blood pressure was low, or she needed more potassium, or her sodium was low. Her condition was up and down like a roller coaster, which was very stressful, but we were pushing her to get better. They were doing physical therapy with her as much as possible—they couldn't do too much of it until the trach was removed. So they would just do exercises in bed with her, trying to get her muscles going again. We couldn't wait to get that trach out. They were constantly monitoring her oxygen, and she was in so much pain from her rheumatoid arthritis. She couldn't sleep at night.

We didn't leave her side. As with the hospital, my brother or I slept at the rehab facility every night, alternating on and off. I wouldn't make him sleep there more than one night in a row, because I felt badly that he had to get up early and work. We were up all night with her. They tried to give her sleeping medicine, but the pain from her rheumatoid arthritis, in addition to back pain, was so awful that it didn't help.

My dad was also there all day, but then my brother would say, "You need to go home and rest." Thank God my oldest daughter, Gia, was around to help with my three younger daughters, especially because the rehab facility was thirty minutes away from my house. Gia was truly amazing through everything. She's the best older sister ever.

Another thing with my mom was that some of the medications they gave her had side effects. She would say crazy things, like, "I see cockroaches. Kill the cockroaches!" or, "I want to go sit right there." I'd say, "Mom, what are you talking about? You can't sit on the floor." I prayed all the time. I would tell everybody to pray for us, even though I really didn't want to talk to a lot of people. Friends wanted to come and see my mom, but she didn't want to see anybody. She was in so much agony that it wasn't like she could just sit there and have a conversation. She would get tired because she was up all night, so often she would sleep during the day. My dad would get frustrated by that, and so would I, because we wanted her to be doing rehab during the day to get her muscles working properly again.

Once they finally took out the trach, we were so happy. Then they started doing a lot more rehab with her, getting her out of bed and encouraging her to walk, but it was hard. She couldn't do it. They would have to hold her up and perform exercises with her. During this time, they moved her to another floor. We took that as a sign of progress. I couldn't wait for her to walk again. I was thinking, *She has to walk again, because if we take her home, she has to be able to at least go to the bathroom by herself.* My father couldn't help her with that and it wasn't realistic for me or my brother to be there at all times. At the rehab facility, they had all the medication and machinery she needed, which made me feel more secure. Everything was right there. If she needed oxygen or sodium or more potassium, right away, they would give it to her. If her blood pressure dropped too low, they would give her blood pressure medicine, because that's what kept happening. They would check her sugar constantly, which was so sad, because some days it was so high because of all the medication that they were pumping into her.

Still, it never crossed our minds that she wouldn't survive. My mom is such a strong woman. I kept saying to her, "I am strong because of you. Look what you've been through." It was a lot. Though, in my heart, I felt she was going to get better. Never in a million years did I think anything else. I told myself, *She is going to walk again. She is going to go home. Positive thinking.* Her doctor was hopeful, too. He was so upbeat, which was amazing. He said, "It's probably going to take a long time, since she's older, but she is going to get there." She was only sixty-six, which didn't seem that old to me, but I was just happy he thought she was going to get better, whenever that happened. So, we waited and kept doing what we were doing every day—being there to support her with whatever she needed.

But, again, there was always something that would set her back. My mom never took care of herself. All her life, she never went to the doctor. She'd only recently started in the past few years because of her rheumatoid arthritis. She always worried about everybody else, and hardly thought about herself. That was just her way, but I tried to stay on top of her. I would even force her to go to the gynecologist. I remember the first time I took her, she said she hadn't gone since Joey was born! She'd insist, "I feel good. Why do I have to go?"

Unfortunately, as it became clear that my mom wasn't going anywhere and things were not improving but actually getting worse, I still had work on the horizon. It was around this time that the casting rumors for the new season of *Real Housewives* began to surface.

I couldn't believe we were starting our eighth season.

For my part, I had no idea who was or wasn't doing the show. Quite honestly, I didn't even care. My focus was on my mom, not on *Real Housewives*.

As it turned out, the producers did reach out to my new yoga buddy Danielle Staub.

Last October, when I was on *Watch What Happens Live*—before they were casting season eight—Andy asked me about it and I told him the truth, which is that Danielle and I were able to pick up right where we'd left off before the table flipping and before I pushed Andy at the reunion! Sorry, honey!

Danielle and I are friends now. We have a lot more in common than I thought. That's what I'm saying about how things evolve. You never know who will come in and out of your life at different stages or for different reasons. I forgave her, she forgave me—just like with me and Melissa. All is good with Danielle and me, which is how it should be. I'm truly thrilled she's on the show.

Another awesome thing that happened in January 2017 was Gia's sweet sixteen. It was a week or so after a very uneventful New Year's Eve—another holiday I wasn't in the mood to celebrate because it just reminded me that Joe had already been in prison for more than nine months—and I was ready to set my sights on something happy and exciting. I could not believe that my baby girl was so grown up. It felt like just yesterday that I'd held her in my arms in the hospital and now she was a woman! Of course I had to throw her a huge bash! I would have anyway, but especially after all the responsibility she'd shouldered while I was away and was still taking on with Joe gone, I wanted to do something for her that she'd never forget. Something that would show her how much I love and appreciate her.

We decided to have it at the Dream Hotel in New York City. I got a party bus to take Gia and about forty of her friends to this insane suite I'd gotten for the night—it had a Jacuzzi in it! They were all dressed up. Gia wore an amazing short grayish-silver dress with cutouts on the sides, and I wore a black dress with a lace-up front. Everyone had an unbelievable time. They played music and I had the hotel cater tons of food and send it to the room, which I'd hired someone to decorate with enormous purple balloons that spelled her name and the number sixteen. There was also an insane, multilayered, bedazzled purple cake with tall candles and cupcakes, too! I bought her the sterling silver Tiffany "T" ring as her gift to match the "T" bracelet I'd gotten her for Christmas. She said it was the best day ever and the best party ever, which gave me endless joy. She deserved every bit of what came to her. She's shouldered a lot of burden these past few years.

I did take a chance and let all the kids—boys and girls—sleep in the suite alone, while Milania, Gabriella, Audriana, and I were in a room next door. You know what, I'm sure people will criticize me for that—what else is new! But my kid is fantastic, and I know in the bottom of my heart that she's responsible and trustworthy. And, of course, I wanted to make her happy. My parents were so strict with me when I was growing up, so I don't want to be that strict with my own girls. There was a time when I did, but I feel differently now. I guess because of what my daughters have been through, I'm a little more lenient than I once was.

Joey and Melissa are much stricter with their kids. When Melissa was a child, her mother wasn't that way, so they're trying to do the opposite, which I respect. Sometimes they condemn my more indulgent attitude, but you know what I say to that: "Don't tell me how to parent, and I won't tell you how to parent. Capiche?"

I'm doing the best I can.

And, as I said, we only get one chance at life.

10

HOW MUCH CAN ONE
HOUSEWIFE TAKE?

a month later, I was excited to start working again, because, listen, I've got to make a living for my kids, especially now, as a single mom. Even though my mom was still very sick, I was okay with it. Of course I would have preferred it if she was home, so I could move forward with a clear head and not take any time away from attending to her, but I had no choice. And, in a sense, it felt nice to have that distraction.

I did feel badly that I couldn't be at the hospital with her all day, every day, but fortunately, we didn't film that much in February and I was able to do what I had to do and then return to my mom immediately. Even my dad said to me, "You have to do it. You have to work for your family." I was also focusing on my yoga. I felt pursuing yoga could lead to more business opportunities. That's the way I'm always thinking. What can I do to support my family, now that I'm the only one standing?

At this point, Danielle was back on the show, which was great, and there was also Margaret Josephs, who was completely new.

Siggy apparently knew her from before we started filming this season. They live in the same town.

For my part, I thought Margaret was a breath of fresh air with her big smile and blond pigtails. She's the founder and designer of a global lifestyle brand, which she launched in 1999, called the Macbeth Collection. They sell clothing, bags, accessories, beauty, home, and tech, all in various colors, prints, and patterns. Right up my alley! She's very talented. She told me that she was sued by Vineyard Vines for a lot of money because they thought she'd tried to copy their logo. *Madonna mia!*

I like Margaret a lot. She's so quick on her feet. She's super sharp and she has good comebacks! What she's accomplished is pretty amazing. I feel like she totally gets me. Like the other day, we were together, just talking, and all of a sudden she looked at me and I felt like she really saw who I was in that moment. I was telling her about my mom and I believe she empathized with everything I've been through. She's also confided in me about the fact that she cheated on her husband with her contractor, whom she's now married to! She was unhappy in her first marriage and she needed to move on. She got that. I used to always say, you can't cheat or you're disgusting. You have to stay with your husband no matter what. I had a singular, uncompromising worldview.

And while I still don't believe that cheating is okay for me or my husband, I now believe that everyone has his or her own set of circumstances. You only get one life, and you have to be happy. You have to be the one who finds that happiness for yourself. Especially after losing my mom, I've come to the conclusion that life is too short to stay miserable. Look, in Margaret's case, she met her new husband in her house. It wasn't like she went looking for him. They ended up falling in love in her own home. It was meant to be. You see what I mean? I feel like everything happens for a reason.

Everybody has this impression of me that I think you have to stay with your man no matter what. Maybe I felt that way at one time, but I don't anymore. You stay with your man *only* if you're happy. People think that I'd never leave Joe. But that's not the case. If Joe frickin' cheats on me or mistreats me, I'm fucking leaving him. I'm not going to stay with him because I'm Italian or because I'm old-school. That's not the way it goes anymore. If things with Joe aren't good or the same between us when he gets home, I'd absolutely end our relationship.

Unexpected things happen in life, I know that now. Look what happened to me. I want to teach people that, never in a million years, did I expect to be in the situation I'm in today. But I know who I am. I know I'm a good person. I still haven't figured out the reason why all these horrible things had to transpire. Who knows? Maybe I'll get my answers when Joe comes home. Maybe I'll see how he is, whether he's changed for the better, and I'll see how our life is together years from now, and then I'll have some comprehension as to why we had to go away. But for now, I don't have any answers yet.

Sure, being in prison altered some of my views of the world. Sure, I'm more forgiving of certain people and extra grateful for certain things. And, yes, I took up yoga, which has helped center me. But, come on, did I really have to be away from my children for eleven and a half whole months to get to this point? I'm sure I could have and would have figured out most of that on my own. Some of these things come naturally with time and age and the new people you encounter who broaden your horizons.

I know I didn't have to go to prison for that long to make all that shit happen. But I did and I took it, because I'm an adult. I can take anything that's thrown at me. I just feel badly for my kids. They were the ones who were punished the most.

That's the part where I say, "Really, God? Explain this to me. I'm all ears."

I just want to find my own happiness, which is why I've learned to be grateful every day for the positive things in my life, like my sweet girls, my family, and the friends who support me.

I have to say, I was impressed by how all the ladies were there for me once we started filming. They knew how difficult it was for me to focus on the show while my mom was in the hospital. Danielle texted me almost every single day. She didn't have to do that. People are busy with their own lives. I get that. Siggy and Dolores were asking for updates on my mother's condition from my lawyer, Jim, with whom they were both speaking. Not only did they care so much, which made me feel really good, but they also understood that it was a time of high stress and that maybe I wouldn't want to be overwhelmed with texts and calls.

But enough about that . . .

February also brought with it Milania's eleventh birthday. When you have a big family, there are a lot of celebrations! We did it at this place called iFLY, which is a facility for controlled, simulated indoor skydiving. It's so cool! You feel like you have wings. We'd been there the previous year—just me, Joe, and the girls. I was terrified the first time because all this air blows up your nose. But we ended up loving it, so Milania wanted to go back for her party. She invited about fifteen of her girlfriends, and I rented them a pink Hummer limousine, which they rode in together, while Gia, Audriana, Gabriella, Gabriella's friend, and I drove separately.

If you haven't been to iFLY, you should totally go. It's an amazing experience! I didn't do it at the party because I was on picture- and video-taking duty, but everyone had a blast. I also bought her a new cell phone as her gift. She said that was what she wanted. All in all, it was a really happy day in the midst of everything going on with my mom.

Just as I was beginning to think things couldn't get any

worse on that front, they did. As I was on my way to go see Joe in prison—I felt badly because I hadn't visited him a lot when my mom was first in the hospital—I got a call from one of the nurses at the rehab facility. I assumed it would be something having to do with my mother, but instead she said, "Your father is having trouble breathing. We have to call an ambulance." I said, "What did you say? My father?" I couldn't believe my own ears.

I turned around immediately and drove to the hospital, where they told me that he had pneumonia. *What the hell?* My brother came to stay with my dad, so I could go back to rehab to be with my mom. After that, Joey and I were never in one place at the same time. It was man-on-man. The only thing I was thankful for was that my mom didn't know my father was sick. And that she seemed fine that day and night. Unfortunately, the next day, her blood pressure dropped and the doctor said, "Something is wrong. She has to go back to the hospital." I couldn't believe it. How much can one family take? Then they checked her lungs and took an X-ray before telling us, "It doesn't look like pneumonia," only for us to find out that it actually *was* pneumonia once we got to the hospital. Apparently, she got pneumonia the second time from my dad, which we did not tell him. We kept everything very quiet, even that my mom had gone back to the hospital. We decided to let him think she was still in rehab, so that his condition wouldn't get any worse. If he'd known what was happening, who knows if he'd have survived it.

So here I am. I spent almost a year in prison. My husband is now there for three years. And *both* my parents are in separate hospitals. My father is at St. Joseph's in Wayne, and my mother is in St. Joseph's in Patterson, which are about five miles away from each other. My mother said she wanted to go to Patterson because it's a trauma center, so they have better machinery. That was her. And she was right: her first day there was better. She was breathing fine. Then, all of a sudden, her breathing became irregular again, and they had to put the breathing tube back in. That's when they put a smaller tube in her mouth, and I said, "Wow, this doesn't look that bad, compared to the first time." On some level, I guess I was getting used to it.

She had the tube in for two or three days before they were able to take it out. She was doing better and, at one point, even got moved up to a floor for patients who are stable. So we were telling my dad that she was fine. We just wanted him to envision her in rehab doing her physical therapy! Joey and I couldn't bear to upset him anymore.

Sometimes, I feel like things happen for a reason. I'm not sure what those reasons are when it comes to everything I've had to endure, but I do know that my father could never have handled seeing what happened to my mother in the last two weeks of her life. He wouldn't have been able to watch her die.

So, I suppose, for that I am grateful.

I've learned you have to find the ray of light in the storm.

11

THE DAY THE MUSIC DIED

*T*he two weeks leading up to my mother's death were the hardest two weeks of my life. Of course, I didn't know what was in store for me, so once they'd taken the breathing tube and trach out and it seemed like she was doing better, I couldn't help but feel optimistic.

One day my brother and I made our parents talk to each other two separate times on the phone. Joey was with my dad and I was with my mom. We knew they needed to hear each other's voices. They were always so in love and barely ever spent a moment apart. Joey and I hoped that by their being able to at least speak to each other, it would help both of them get better. My father needed to know that my mother was doing okay. Remember, he still thought she was in the rehab facility, and my mother had no idea my father was in the hospital—thank God they didn't put two and two together!

Soon after that, there was one night when my mom slept straight through without waking up in pain. It was the first peaceful rest I could remember her having, with the exception of a singular night a while back when the Ambien they'd given her actually worked. That's what would happen, any given medication would work the first time they gave it to her and then, beyond that, it would make her hallucinate and say crazy things.

So that night, she slept all night. I kept looking at her. You know, like when you're checking on a newborn baby to see if his or her chest is rising and falling. I thought, *She never sleeps all night. What's the problem?* The next morning, her blood pressure dropped again and the doctor said, "We have to bring her back to the ICU. She has an infection." I said, "An infection? Are you sure? She had a great night. She finally slept!" And they said, "That's what happens when you have an infection, it makes you sleep." They brought her back to the ICU and found out she had sepsis. They didn't know where it came from. The only thing they could think, was that it might have come from the PICC line in her neck. She was in so much pain that whole day because of it. I was scared, because sepsis can be life-threatening, yet I still thought she was going to be okay.

Sepsis can also cause confusion, so once she had it, she started saying some crazy stuff. She was telling me she wanted her own mom to come get her. My maternal grandmother passed away when my mother was twelve years old. She also mentioned her uncle Antonio in Italy, and I was thinking, *Oh my God, what the hell is happening?* She was asking for my brother all the time, so I called Joey and said, "You need to leave Dad and come to this hospital. She wants you here. You are not leaving the whole day; you need to stay with us." And he did. My mother has always had a special place in her heart for my brother. Sons are different. They're not with their mothers a lot like daughters are—I saw my mom almost every day when she was alive—so she was continually asking for him. My mom adored Joey. Of course, she adored me, too, but it was different with my brother, which is kind of funny, because my dad definitely likes girls better!

We both slept there with our mom for two nights, and then my brother said, "You are going home today. You've got to go be with your kids." I knew he was right. I went home to my girls, knowing that she was in capable, loving hands.

So, my brother slept there with her, and when I called him in the morning, he said, "It was a bad night." We would always call each other in the morning to check in on both of our parents. I said, "I have to get the kids to school. I'll be over soon," because Joey had to leave for a little bit to go set up his guys on one of his jobs. Before I could get to the hospital, I got a call from one of the nurses saying that my mother had stopped breathing for a few seconds, her blood pressure had dropped, and she'd gone into cardiac arrest. I said, "WHAT?!" My whole body started shaking, and my heart was beating at my chest. They said, "You need to get here right now." I honestly thought *I* might have a heart attack. I get the chills just thinking about it.

The best way to explain it is that it felt like an out of body experience. The kids were still home, so I said to them, "You have to take the bus to school today. I can't drive you. I've got to go now." And, with that, I rushed to the hospital. I was driving like a maniac. I was even driving on the shoulder at some points. I called my brother from the car and told him what had happened. I said, "Joey, you need to get there. Mommy stopped breathing for a few seconds."

Once we arrived, she was back on the breathing tube again. They told us they'd given her a medication to try to alleviate the pain, because it was so horrible. I'm telling you, every medication they gave her didn't work. I don't understand why, but—if you can believe it—I still thought she was going to be okay. I thought she would eventually come home to us.

That's when they told us that she'd stopped producing urine. When you don't produce urine, you have to go on dialysis. That's also when things really began going downhill, even though I didn't realize it at the time. They asked me, "Do you want her to do dialysis?" And I said yes. I wanted them to keep trying everything. So they put a line through her leg and attempted, but it didn't work. They said, "We can't even do it. Her blood pressure is dropping." They had her on *four* different medications for blood pressure and still couldn't get the line

Celebrating Audriana's First Communion with her godmother, Dina Manzo. She told me that day that she and her boyfriend, Dave, were engaged. I was beyond excited for them! I love, love, love Dina. She's beautiful inside and out and just the sweetest, most authentic person. All I want is to see her happy.

Here I am with my father at the opening of our family's brand-new restaurant in East Hanover, New Jersey, called Gorga's Homemade Pasta & Pizza, which was inspired by my mother. It was a very proud night for all of us.

This was my mom's sixty-sixth birthday. I had no idea it would be the last one I would ever spend with her. It's heartbreaking just to think about that. I am glad, though, that we had such a nice celebration for her at Joey and Melissa's house. We all had dinner together—me and my kids, my mom, my dad, Joey, Melissa, and their kids. My parents cooked together, even though it was my mom's special day. They loved to be in control of the cooking!

The girls loved celebrating their big sister's Sweet 16. We did the décor in all purple. Gia said it was the best night and party ever, which made me so happy.

We celebrated Gia's confirmation with a beautiful and delicious cake by the Cake Boss, Buddy Valastro. Gia has grown into such a remarkable young woman.

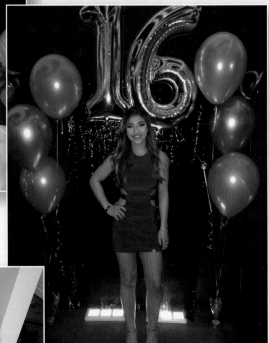

I can't believe my baby Gia turned Sweet 16! We had her party at the Dream Hotel in New York City.

Gia looked so gorgeous before the prom! Her dress is by Jacqueline Boutique in Livingston, NJ.

Audriana showing her American pride by posing as Olympic gold medalist Laurie Hernandez at an event at school. I was so proud of her for picking such a great role model.

I love going to Audriana's dance competitions. She's so amazing on stage. I wish I was that flexible!

Audriana did a "wax museum" project at school where everyone had to pick someone they wanted to grow up to be like, and they had to replicate that person. She said she wanted to be Laurie Hernandez, who was part of the US women's gymnastics team that won the gold medal in the 2016 Summer Olympics.

My gorgeous Audriana on her First Holy Communion. She wore the most stunning white dress, which she designed herself at Little Nikki's boutique in Ho-Ho-Kus, New Jersey. It was sleeveless and had an enormous puffy white skirt with all sorts of embellishments, like flowers and crystals. Her hair was in the sweetest ringlets. She looked like a Disney princess!

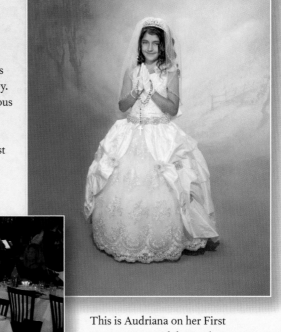

This is Audriana on her First Communion with her godparents, Dina Manzo and our close family friend John. Dina flew in from California; she's like a sister to me.

Audriana's First Communion was such a special day. I wore cutout white lace pants that had white shorts underneath and a white lace spaghetti strap top by Nicole Miller that I absolutely loved. We had an amazing cake, which was in the shape of a huge white cross with big white flowers on it and edible gold rosary beads. Piped in gold icing, it read, "God Bless Audriana 05•13•2017."

I work hard to maintain a strong, healthy body, so I felt great during this girls' weekend in Boca Raton, Florida.

I had so much fun doing an appearance and spending time with my girlfriends at the Wynn in Las Vegas. What happens in Vegas stays in Vegas!

Here I am outside Milan Cathedral in May 2017. After losing my mother, this journey to Italy felt like a pilgrimage. I was destined to be as close to her as I could possibly be.

This was the night I saw "Jennifer Lopez: All I Have" at Planet Hollywood Resort & Casino in Las Vegas. It was one of the best shows I've ever seen, and it was so great to meet her that night. She's even more beautiful in person!

With my oldest daughter, Gia, on the day of her confirmation.

I was so proud of my baby Gia for an amazing weekend at her cheer competition in Myrtle Beach, South Carolina. They placed first. What an achievement!

My beautiful daughter Gia on her confirmation. God bless her. I love her so much.

My girls are everything to me. I loved celebrating my forty-fifth birthday with them!

With my father at the opening of Gorga's Homemade Pasta & Pizza. It really was such a fun party. We served homemade pasta, which we made right on the premises.

Love my brother, Joey! This was us celebrating my forty-fifth birthday. Melissa got me the ugliest zebra print cake. I said, "You're kidding me, right? I put you in charge of this one thing, and this is what you get?" Then she joked, "You, me, and desserts just don't go good together," in reference to the sprinkle-cookie incident. *Madonna mia!*

in any higher. She was so swollen because they'd pumped her with all this medication. It was absolutely awful.

My brother came, then Melissa, and then Gia. I'd told the girls not to come to the hospital, even Gia. I'd said, "I don't want you to go through this. Nonna is going to go," but she came. She insisted. Her boyfriend, Nick, brought her. Then my other kids wanted to see her, but I just felt like it wasn't the right thing. It would have been too much. Everyone was a wreck. My mother kept saying to us, "Tell your father that I love him," and I kept saying to her, "No, you are going to be fine, Ma. You are fine." Other times, she would just say that she couldn't take it anymore. She would say, "Pull the plug," and I'd reply, "Ma, there is no plug here. Stop saying that." I knew my mom would never want to live her life hooked up to a machine. I was heartbroken.

Eventually, they took the breathing tube out and the doctor said, "There's nothing else that we can do. It's going to happen." We all just held hands—with her, with each other—and spoke to her. That was all we could do. We embraced her and kissed her. She was kind of out of it, but we were still saying things to her. We sobbed nonstop. It didn't feel real. I just sat there looking at her. *My mother.* I didn't want to say goodbye. I didn't think she was ever going to leave me. My brother said he wishes that he knew she was going before the very end. That if he'd known he would have said certain things to her. It was all so sudden. This woman who had been everything to all of us was leaving us in an instant. How do you say goodbye to someone like that? She was so young. So full of life. Until she wasn't.

We stayed with her for more than an hour, just crying our eyes out. It didn't feel like long enough, but we knew that, at some point, we had to let go. Despite the unimaginable sadness, I was so happy that I could be by her side while she took her last breaths—for myself and for her. Walking back to the car was a complete blur. The only thing I remember thinking was that I couldn't believe my mother was no longer on this earth. When your grief is that deep, it's hard to wrap your mind around anything else. It was truly surreal.

March 3, 2017, was the last day I got to see my mother alive.

I couldn't believe that my dad wasn't there and didn't know anything about what was going on. We were numb and also terrified to tell our father. Joey and I kept saying to each other, "How are we going to tell Daddy?" We truly thought that there was a chance he might die when we told him. We were sick to our stomachs. We were going out of our minds. My whole body was trembling.

We didn't tell my father that night. We couldn't. All we wanted to do was go home and lie in bed and cry. I had to tell my other three daughters, which was heart-wrenching for all of us, and I didn't sleep at all that night. I just went through the motions, because I was completely numb.

The next day my brother picked me up. We actually had Gia come, too, because my father adores her, and she wanted to be there. Also she was his first grandchild, so we felt like maybe he would be strong because she was there. Joey and I were completely petrified, because we knew that this was going to be a shock to our father. Here he was in the hospital and he believed that his wife was still in the rehab facility getting better. We went to get some breakfast first, because I couldn't remember the last time I'd sat down for an actual meal. My brother said, "You've got to eat something. You've got to be strong for your kids. You can do this." So, we went for breakfast, and then we met the lung doctor at the hospital, because we thought, God forbid we tell our dad and he stops breathing. We wanted his doctor in the room with us for safe measure.

You have to understand that the staff at St. Joseph's in Wayne, where my father was, all knew that my mother was at St. Joseph's in Patterson. But *nobody* told him. We made them swear not to. There was one day, when a doctor slipped and said, "I just saw your wife in Patterson," and my dad got so upset that his blood pressure went sky-high. Fortunately, he later got confused and forgot about it. That was when my mother had been taken off the breathing tube and we made them talk, so it worked out well.

Anyway, the doctor was due to meet us at St. Joseph's in Wayne at 8:00 a.m. Joey and I felt like little kids: we were terrified to make our dad upset. It hadn't been an easy decision to keep him in the dark the whole time. We just figured there was no point to worry him and possibly make him sicker, since our mother was going to return to rehab and ultimately get better. I wish our hopes had been reality. Even though she was back and forth between the hospital and rehab, and the status of her health was very up and down, there really was no indication that she was going to die until the very end. So, what was better: not telling him, and then if, God forbid things go south, shock him with the news? Or telling him, just in case she did die, and unnecessarily stress him out, since he could not be there by her bedside? There was no right answer. We did the best we could. Through everything I've endured, I've learned that's all you can do.

Next to seeing my mom pass away, telling my father that the love of his life was gone was the second hardest thing I've ever had to do. The entire car ride to the hospital, Joey and I were just trying to figure out the best way to do that. Fortunately—or maybe unfortunately—he did that job for us.

As soon as Joey and I walked into his room, he said, "Where is my wife?" That was the first thing out of his mouth—not even hello. He knew something was up, because my brother and I had never been to visit him together. How could we? My brother would stay with my dad, and I would stay with my mom, or vice versa. We were, literally, never in the same place at the same time, except with my mother in the end.

Right away, we all started crying and hugging him.

Joey said, "Papa, now she is free. She was in so much pain.

She was suffering. Now she can run." We sometimes call my father Papa, because he likes it better than Daddy.

My dad shook his head and said, "I didn't get to say goodbye." So I told him, "Papa, I think Mommy planned it this way. She didn't want you to see her suffer." I really believe that. I think, like us, she knew that he wouldn't have been able to handle seeing her pass away. I said, "Mommy didn't want you to see her leave. She never wanted you to see her leave. Joey and I were there. It's just the way she wanted it." He kept saying, "I want to see my wife." He was inconsolable.

We cried all day. We didn't leave him. I slept there that night.

We decided not to have a showing at my mom's funeral. I didn't want the kids to go through that. Only my dad wanted to see her. We had to pick out her dress and everything, which was something I hadn't thought about. She wore the dress that she wore to my wedding, which she always loved. Even her best friend told me it was her favorite. She said she'd always wanted to make it shorter, so she could wear it somewhere else, but that she just never got around to it. It was gray silk underneath and then black lace over it, to complement my bridal party, who wore mercury gray. She looked so gorgeous that day. I was so happy that she got to wear it again, but—at the same time—I had this huge pit in my stomach. You never think about having to dress someone after they've passed away, so while it felt like the right choice, it was bittersweet and painful all at once.

I'd never arranged a funeral before, so this was all new for me. My brother was the one who went to the mausoleum to find her spot. He called us on FaceTime, so he could show us the options. We selected something at eye level and then Joey picked the casket.

I can't explain how strange the whole thing felt. When I was at home, I kept thinking, *Why am I here? I'm supposed to be with my mother. I need to be with her.* I was driving myself crazy. For the past three months, I'd been so accustomed to being with her all day, every day, with the exception of a few minutes here or there to take the kids to school or their activities or when I was filming. I would literally run out of the hospital to get things done, and run right back as fast as I possibly could. And now she was in the hospital all alone, waiting to be buried. To me that was devastating. I just paced back and forth in my house. My legs were shaking. Joe's family came over, which was nice. But they were just looking at me, because they didn't know what to say or what to do. I didn't want to cry or scream with other people there. That's not my way.

I just wanted to be left alone.

My nerves were shot.

My mother was gone forever.

I posted a passage called "Your Mother Is Always With You" two weeks after she died. Here are a few lines that spoke to me and everything I was feeling. There aren't many moments I am rendered speechless, too numb to function. This was one of them.

YOUR MOTHER IS ALWAYS WITH YOU.

She's the cool hand on your brow when you're not feeling well. She's your breath in the air on a cold winter's day. She is the sound of the rain that lulls you to sleep, the colors of a rainbow.

She is Christmas morning.

Your mother lives inside your laughter. She's crystallized in every teardrop. She's the place you came from, your first home, and she's the map you follow with every step you take. She's your first love; your first friend, even your first enemy, but nothing on earth can separate you. Not time, not space, and not even death.

—*Author Unknown*

12

THE AFTERMATH

/n recent years I've had my share of difficult days. I've had days where I've woken up and hated my life. Days when I've asked myself how I was going to remain strong. For myself, and for my family. There are more of those days than I can count on both hands.

But those days were *nothing* compared to the day we buried my mother.

Not being sentenced to prison, not going to prison, nothing.

It was truly the worst day of my entire life.

After my mother passed away, it felt like I was surrounded by a thick fog. I was receiving so many texts and voice mails from friends offering their condolences that I literally had to shut my phone off.

I could not talk to anyone.

My biggest fear was that my father wouldn't be released in time for my mother's funeral, which was scheduled for the Monday after she left us. We'd made all the arrangements quickly because my dad had told us that they said he would be ready to go on Sunday—so of course we listened to him, which we shouldn't have, especially since that's not exactly what the staff had told him! He hated being in the hospital. Who doesn't?

The doctor actually got mad at us. He said, "Your father is not prepared to leave." That sent me into a full-on panic. I said, "What are you talking about? My dad can not miss my mother's funeral!" I was thinking, *Do I need to change everything now? All of our family and friends have already made arrangements!* We told the doctor that everything was scheduled for Monday morning. But he remained firm and informed us, "I need to see how he's doing first. Otherwise, I am not discharging him." We said, "We thought he was doing better." He said, "No. His oxygen level has to stay up. If it doesn't stay up, he's not getting out of the hospital."

I was in such a state. I had no idea what to do. My father didn't end up leaving the hospital until eight thirty on Monday morning, and we had to be at the church by ten o'clock. We were all flipping out. All he had time to do was go home and take a shower. My brother helped him get ready. Fortunately, the funeral home was right next door to their house. Joey picked it for that reason, which was smart.

Thank God a friend of ours who's a doctor was able to get

my dad a wheelchair because he needed it. There was no way he was going to be able to walk or stand through all that. They had him on an oxygen tank, too. Can you imagine? It was absolutely unthinkable, but I was just grateful that he'd been released. I don't know what we would have done otherwise.

Once that nightmare was over, when it came time for the funeral itself, I was in a complete daze. I honestly had no idea what was going on around me. The details are a blur. I was beside myself. Out of everything that had happened to me and to my family, losing my mother was perhaps the biggest shock of all. I expected to have another thirty years with her, at least. I needed her to be there for me and for my girls. And I couldn't imagine living in a world without her in it. *Who would I call a million times a day? Who would help me take care of my daughters while Joe was in prison, and even after he came home? Who would cook Sunday suppers with me? Who would be my rock? Who would hold us all together?*

I had so many unanswered questions. Above all, though, I suppose I just felt like it was unfair that she'd been taken away from us at such a young age, particularly when she had so much more to give. Again, I couldn't help but wonder, *Why me? What did I do to deserve yet another tragedy?*

Even though my mother had died, sadly, it didn't mean that I could stop working. The Bravo cameras were there the day of the funeral, filming. They were very respectful and remained as far away as they could, in order to give us our privacy and space. I don't remember being asked about it, but it didn't bother me. I was numb anyway. My brother was happy that they were there. He made a good point in saying that, since we were so out of it that day, it would be nice to have it on tape so we could go back and look at it in a few months or a few years when—if we were lucky—the sting of losing her wouldn't be so fresh. And we wouldn't be as raw from the incredible pain.

I believe Bravo is going to do a tribute to our mother on the show, as they did with Joe's father, which is really nice. We think about our mom multiple times every day, so I think it'll be special to have that experience documented, even though saying goodbye to her was the saddest moment in all our lives.

I'd go to prison again just to have her back.

The one thing I do remember about that day was that I was trying to be strong and hold it together for my kids and for my father. And, in a strange sense, for my mother, too. Because she was the strongest person I've ever known and I felt like she wouldn't want me to be a mess on the outside, even though I was a wreck on the inside. That's one way I am like my mother—I don't like to break down in front of other people. I prefer to put on a brave face and push through.

Not to mention that I wanted to be there for my dad, who was devastated. Since he'd just come out of the hospital that morning, he wasn't himself. He was very weak. And, again, he was on oxygen and in a wheelchair. It was truly awful to watch, but nothing would have gotten in the way of my dad being there. He needed to see my mom and to say goodbye to his wife of forty-seven years. I can't even wrap my head around being married to someone for that long. They were a part of each other. My parents were even more passionate about each other in the end than they were in the beginning. Now that's a true love story.

So, anyway, we went to church. Then from the church we went to the mausoleum. As a final goodbye to my mom, everyone released dozens of white balloons into the sky. I shared a video of it on Instagram set to Wiz Khalifa and Charlie Puth's, "See You Again" with the caption: *Clear skies all the way to HEAVEN for my Mommy. I Love You.* #loveforamom.

After the mausoleum we had a repast luncheon with our closest friends and family at an Italian restaurant called Spiga, in Totowa, New Jersey. There were appetizers, entrées, pasta, salad, and dessert. Lots and lots of food. That's what my father wanted. He didn't want a ton of people to come back to my house. It would have been too much.

Everyone was trying to keep my father uplifted. His sister, Maria, came, which was really significant, since they hadn't spoken in years. Her daughter and son—and my cousins—Rosie and Anthony came. Anthony's wife and son were also there. We all put our differences aside for the day. It was like nothing bad had ever happened. We just picked up where we'd left off. Although Anthony's sister—and my other cousin—Kathy Wakile (and her husband, Richie), who'd been one of the *Housewives* with me in seasons past, did not come, nor did her other two brothers. Kathy's excuse was that she was in Florida. Can you believe that? How hard is it to come home from Florida? It's so close, and the tickets are cheap. What are they, two hundred dollars? *Come on.* Kathy ended up stopping by when she got back. But, for me, that was too little too late. I was very disappointed. And, to be honest, disgusted.

Outside of family, I'd asked Lisa G. to tell only my closest friends about the service, as I didn't want my mother's funeral to turn into a circus.

Despite what people may think, I have a very small and tight-knit group of girlfriends.

The two Lisas were there, Lisa F. and her husband and Lisa G. along with her mother and brother. My friends John and Kim were there. Rosana and Jackie. Rose and Leah and Robyn and Christina. Rino and Teresa Aprea also came.

Lucilla D'Agostino, the executive producer of the show, along with Dorothy Toran and Jacob Huddleston, two other executives on the show were there. Jim and his wife, Rebecca. My makeup artist and friend Priscilla DiStasio. Siggy and her husband, Michael, and Dolores and her ex-husband, Frank. Danielle didn't come. I think maybe she felt weird about it since we'd just become friends again. We'd only seen each other a handful of times. I wasn't upset by that at all. I think she did what was appropriate, and I appreciated that she didn't try to insert herself into a situation just to be on camera or because she wanted to see what was going on. If the circumstances had been reversed, I probably wouldn't have gone to her mother's funeral, either. So no judgment there.

A lot of Joey and Melissa's friends came, as did Joe's entire family and many members of Melissa's family.

There were so many others who were there, each of them helping to ease the pain on this very difficult day.

I couldn't believe it when I looked up and saw Dina Manzo and her boyfriend, Dave, there. Dina later told me that she had called Jim and that he'd given her the information so she could book her flight out from Malibu. The fact that she flew all the way from California to be with my family on this day meant the world to me.

Dina also posted this beautiful note on Instagram, accompanied by a photo of my mom and me. It really touched me.

My heart bleeds for my girlfriend and her family . . . Teresa and I have been friends since we were 22yrs old. Over the years I've had the pleasure to get to know & love her beautiful mother. Such a warm yet strong woman. I had an immense respect for her as a woman, wife, mother and Grandmother. Often times in the height of the Real Housewives drama she would hug me extra tight goodbye and thank me for never turning on her daughter. She would tell me I was a "good girl" and much like my own parents I never wanted to disappoint her. I got to spend many special Sunday dinners with her while Teresa was away. She would always make sure I had extra salad or would jump up and boil more pasta because I didn't eat meat. Just like a mama does. I'll cherish

those memories. ~May she rest easy . . . my girl now has the
ultimate Angel watching over her in this most difficult time
in her life.

When I finally turned my phone back on, I had literally hundreds of text messages, voice mails, and emails.

One of them was from Jacqueline Laurita.

After all we had been through, it was nice of her to reach out, but I was happy that neither she nor Caroline showed up in person, even though they did come to the wake when Joe's father passed away. I ignored Jacqueline's text. It may have been a nice sentiment, but I don't think that people should reach out at a time like that. I really don't. If we're not friends and you don't speak to me on a regular basis, why touch base when tragedy strikes? It feels so fake.

I did ask my lawyer Jim to get permission for Joe to leave prison for the day so he could be there. The prison system allows that under certain circumstances. He was completely devastated when I told him about my mom; he cried hysterically. Joe adored my mother. If the funeral had been Wednesday, he might have been able to be there, but it all happened so fast that there wasn't enough time to do the proper paperwork. I was okay with it, because—once I thought about it— I didn't think it would help my kids. I figured it would be more emotionally stressful for them. I didn't want them to feel like Daddy was out of prison and might be able to come home with us. So it worked out for the best. It was a hard enough day for them as it was, having to say goodbye to their grandmother. I told them all to write a letter to her, and we put them in her coffin. It was the first time Gabriella, Milania, and Audriana had been to a funeral. Gia had come when my father-in-law died, which was a lot because he had a full wake. Two hours, which was torture. I could barely sit there. I like the way Jewish people do it. Nobody has to see anything.

My brother bought two spots at the cemetery. One for my mom and one for my dad, so, eventually, they'll be together forever again, which is perfect. My dad goes to visit her every single day. I was going with him, and the kids, too, but on days that I'm working, sometimes it's impossible to get there.

My dad lives with us now. He came to stay with me immediately. We couldn't let him live alone at first, because he was on oxygen. We would go pick up stuff for him, like his clothes and anything else he needed, and then one day he said, "I can't live in that house without her. It's too hard." They had just recently moved there over the summer in order to downsize, but he said, "Even though there are not a lot of memories there, I still see her everywhere I look." He couldn't stay. And with Joe gone, it seemed like the best decision for everyone.

Beyond the agonizing progression of losing my mother, I was also scared to find out what my life would look like without her. Sometimes when you're so consumed by the course of losing a loved one—first they get sick, then their condition worsens, and ultimately they pass away—you don't think about how you're going to feel when the dust settles. When all the people stop calling and coming by, and things go back to the status quo. Only, it's not the status quo as you know it, because one of the most major pieces of your existence is gone. Just like that.

My mom was the glue that bound us. I'm not saying that fathers aren't important. Of course they are. But mothers are different. I see that now. Women are stronger than men are. They just are. I see it with my husband. I see it with my dad. They can't handle half the stuff that my mother could or I can. Women are pretty amazing.

I still talk to my mom all the time. I'll say things like, "Ma, please let Daddy's nose stop bleeding so I don't have to take him back to the hospital." Or "Ma, please watch over us and make sure all the girls stay happy and healthy." I believe she's taking care of us from heaven. I know she's up there smiling and laughing, and probably wishing she could reprimand me for a few things! I also know that one day we'll all be together again.

Of course I wish Joe had been around to support me—to support all of us—during such a heart-wrenching time in our lives. We hadn't seen each other in so long, because I was in my own world dealing with my mom and my dad. I couldn't go visit him. And I didn't even want to. Nothing else mattered to me aside from my mother's and father's health. Plus, I had all the kids' birthdays and activities. I was going to soccer and gymnastics and a bunch of Gia's cheerleading competitions. I put my parents and my children in front of everything. Joe simply wasn't my top priority—far from it. Not to mention that it takes a whole day to go see him, and my daughters were going with Joe's mother anyway, so that worked out well. Even if I can't get there, it's very important to me that they can. No matter what my situation is with my husband, he's the girls' father, and they need to see their father as often as possible.

To be honest, I don't like going to prison, even just on visitation. I thought I was done with that! I don't like being in that big room with everyone. I don't want people looking at us or listening to what we say. I don't need anyone else in my business. I was going to go see Joe after my mom died, but then they found contraband in someone's room and the prison stopped visitations for twenty-one days. They punished the whole facility for one person's crime—that's how it goes sometimes. After that, there was another chicken pox outbreak, so they banned visitation during that time, too.

By this point, it had really started to feel like we were estranged. I missed being hugged. I needed to be held. I needed someone there with me! I was there for him when his dad died, and I remember just caressing and holding him. I didn't get that. I was taking care of my dad and my kids. I was responsible for all of us. And, the thing is, when everyone you know is grieving, there's no one left to be there for you.

But, as I always say, God only gives us what we can handle. I think God has been pushing the limit with me, though. Sometimes, I feel like screaming, "What the hell? I need a break. I want things to be good. I can't wait for things to just be normal again."

There are still moments that, when the phone rings, I expect it to be my mom calling, because I used to speak to her twenty times a day. There are other moments when I think it's going to be her walking through my front door. We were as close as a mother and daughter could be. She was like my sister and my best friend all in one.

There came a point at which I got angry; the second stage of grief. I thought, *Life sucks*, because you get so busy and wrapped up with everything going on around you—your kids, your work, your friends, and the days just go by. Then you regret not spending more time with the person before they passed away. And, of course, in my case, I'd been in prison for almost a year, so that made it even worse. I could have been with my mom during that time instead. All I could think was, *Why now? Why my mom? Why did she have to die?* My kids lost their mother for eleven and a half months, their father for three years, their paternal grandfather, and now their beloved *nonna* was gone, too. Audriana is still having a tough time with it. She'll start crying and say, "I miss Nonna." It's really hard to hear that.

But, despite the searing pain, I do know one thing. My mother was proud of me and the woman I've become. All of her friends—anyone she spoke to—tells me that my mom praised me constantly. She lived and breathed for me and my brother. Still, that doesn't change the fact that I wanted more time with her.

I miss my mom every second of every minute of every day.

Rest in peace, Ma.

IN MEMORY OF
ANTONIA GORGA
October 20, 1950–March 3, 2017

She always leaned to watch for us,
anxious if we were late,
in the winter by the window,
in the summer by the gate;
and though we mocked her tenderly,
who had such foolish care,
the long way home would seem more
safe because she waited there.
Her thoughts were all so full of us—
she never could forget!
And so I think that where she is
she must be watching yet,
waiting till we come home to her,
anxious if we are late—
watching from heaven's window,
leaning from heaven's gate.

13

LIFE GOES ON . . .

*T*he weeks after my mother died went by in a blur. All I really remember is trying to stay strong for my kids and my father, while stealing private moments to allow myself to cry. I'd never lost someone so important in my life—the *most* important person in my life, next to my children. It's an experience I wish on no one. Not even my worst enemy. My mom had such a good soul. Everyone she interacted with loved her. But I needed her. I mean, I really, really needed her with everything I was going through. And, just like that, she was gone. It was so fast. So gut-wrenching.

I don't always understand why God works the way he does. Or why he took my mother from us at such an early age, when she had so much life left in her and so much left to give. I kept thinking, *I just want to talk to her one last time. I want to give her one more hug and one more kiss.* I wanted that for my father, too. He didn't even have the chance to see her or speak to her before she died, which I knew was eating away at him, even though it was probably for the best.

We were all in deep mourning. And we needed something to liven us up.

When I'd thought that my mother was going to pull through, I'd scheduled a trip for all of us to go to Puerto Rico, since we'd never made it to Punta Cana in December. I figured we'd finally have the chance to take the vacation we all so desperately needed. To be together as a family and just kick back and relax. As I mentioned, my mother loved, loved, loved the beach. She couldn't get enough of it! Same with my father and with me.

Even though my mother couldn't come with us, we decided to go anyway. I knew she would have wanted us to. And, let's be honest, we all really, really needed to get away and escape reality for a little while. So I took my girls, my friends, and my dad. I knew I had to do some filming for *Real Housewives* while I was there, but I'm used to that, so I didn't care. I was just so happy to get out of town for a change.

I wasn't sure how the mood would be, given that everyone was still so sad, but I was happy that we all ended up having the best time. The resort was gorgeous and had spectacular views of the beach. We went snorkeling and kayaking. We rode Jet Skis® and went paddleboarding, which the kids loved! We even went zip-lining, which I was so freakin' scared to do, but I overcame my fear and did it. I was super proud of myself and also of my girls for being brave. If there's one thing I've learned it's that you need to be courageous, hold your head high, and take risks sometimes.

We also had some beautiful meals while we were in Puerto Rico, and one night we roasted s'mores over this huge fire pit. Overall it was an amazing bonding experience for me and my daughters, for me and my friends, and for the girls and their *nonno*. We all missed my mother very much. When I got home, in honor of her, I posted this on Instagram:

Death changes everything! Time changes nothing. . . . I still miss the sound of your voice, the wisdom in your advice, the stories of your life and just being in your presence. So no, time changes nothing, I miss you as much today as I did the day you died. I just miss you!

The day after we got home from Puerto Rico was Easter. If I'd known that my mom was going to pass away, I would have planned to stay on vacation through Sunday. But when I booked the trip, I still thought she was going to pull through and be able to come with us. So I figured we'd come back on Saturday and then be able to spend Easter Sunday together at home, as a family, the way we normally do.

Typically, either I host Easter at my house or Joey and Melissa do it at their house; that's how it is with most of the holidays. We organize an egg hunt for all the kids. And we cook and eat, which isn't a surprise! We usually make lasagna and Italian pizza with ricotta and eggs. We all try to dress up, too; the kids wear hats and pretty dresses. I always put together big baskets for them with chocolate bunnies and eggs and stuff like that.

This year, though, things were much more low-key. Since we'd just come home from Puerto Rico, I had to run out first thing Sunday morning and buy all the kids' baskets so they'd be there when they woke up in the morning. After that, we didn't do much. It was just like a regular Sunday. I didn't want to do anything. My dad didn't want to do anything. We wanted it to go by like any other day, because my mother couldn't be with us. I took Gia to her boyfriend's house, and then I took my other three daughters to Joe's family's house so they were able to spend time with them. I just went home and hung out with my dad. We relaxed and watched TV, and my brother went to see Melissa's family. We did have family dinner together as usual, but I wasn't in a celebratory mood.

While the vacation had been a welcome distraction from my mom, returning to normal made it even more difficult not to dwell on her being gone. I know Easter is a holy day that represents resurrection, but all I could feel was profound loss. A pit in my stomach that I couldn't fill no matter how hard I tried. A few days later, I posted the following poem, because it captured my emotions so well. I know it may seem silly or pointless to share these kinds of things publicly, but—in a way—it offers me a sense of relief since I'm used to bottling everything up. Also, I know there are many people who've lost their moms or their dads or someone close to them. If I can help even one of those people get through the hard times like I am, or if even one of those people takes solace in the same words that I do, then it's worth it. I've learned it's so important to open yourself up. No matter how painful that might be. It's the only way to begin to heal.

They say there is a reason,
They say that time will heal,
But neither time nor reason,
Will change the way I feel,
For no-one knows the heartache,
That lies behind my smile,
No-one knows how many times,
I have broken down and cried,
I want to tell you something,
So there won't be any doubt,
You're so wonderful to think of,
But so hard to be without.

—Author Unknown

14

THE MOTHERLAND

I almost didn't make it on the *Real Housewives* season eight trip to Milan. Yup, you heard me right. It was touch and go until a few hours before the plane took off. But let's backtrack for a moment.

On the Saturday night before I was supposed to leave for Italy on Monday, I had to rush my father to the hospital. It had been a long hard day of work, which I'd capped off by attending a Cinco de Mayo party at a friend of a friend's house in Connecticut. I was hoping to finally relax and have fun, which I did. I was planning to sleep over and return home early in the morning, but—for some reason—I made the last-minute decision to drive back to New Jersey. Someone must have been looking down on me! Because at around three o'clock in the morning, my dad woke me up to tell me that his nose was bleeding and it wouldn't stop. So off we went to the hospital, where they were able to get it under control. Phew!

Unfortunately, that wasn't the end of it. The following morning it started up again. We kept waiting to see if it would stop bleeding—my father *hates* the hospital even more than the average person, especially since he spends so much time there—but no luck. It would stop bleeding for a few minutes and then start right back up. By 11:00 a.m. we were at the hospital again. We were there for a few hours, because these things always seem to take forever. Finally, they put some kind of rock thing in his nostrils to plug them and said we were free to leave. Again, phew!

Or not.

Back at home his nose was bleeding on and off. And, then, to make matters worse, he started spitting up blood clots from the blood dripping down his throat. They were enormous. I kept saying, "Oh my God, Dad! Do we need to go to the hospital again?" I mean, I could look down his throat and see the blood coming up. And then, almost immediately, the plug from his nose fell out, too. But my father was insistent that this was normal, because that's what they'd told us at the hospital, so we waited.

I hadn't packed a thing yet for Italy, and I had about twenty-four hours before I had to leave. I started throwing things in my suitcases, trying to figure out what I'd need for all the different activities they'd planned for us, all the dinners and nights out, and all the scenes we were going to film. It may sound silly, but it's a lot to think about and it's stressful. It's much different than when you're just going on a vacation with your family. Not only did I have to think about what I wanted to wear in terms of clothing, but I had to consider shoes, jewelry, and other accessories. Plus makeup and toiletries. I was so anxious. It was the last thing I wanted to do when my father wasn't feeling well.

The whole time I was packing, I kept checking on him and he kept saying he was fine. A couple of hours later, we had our usual Sunday Italian dinner and everything seemed to be going as smoothly as possible. I should have known that was too good to be true!

Because at 3:00 a.m—just a few hours after I'd picked up Gia at the airport—we were back at the hospital again. No joke. This time, my father was having trouble breathing, in addition to his nosebleed and the fact that he was coughing up blood. You have to understand that my dad has a lot of health issues, so while I was definitely concerned, this wasn't that out of the ordinary for us. My dad is amazing, God bless him. He's such a strong guy. So strong that even though he was enduring all of this, he kept saying, "Don't worry about me. It's just blood. I'm fine." Really Dad? I don't think so.

After what happened with my mom, my motto is: *You can never be too careful.* I sleep in the family room with him every night. There's a pullout bed for me, and my father sleeps on the couch. I'd be more than happy to take the couch and give him the bed, but he doesn't like the bed because of his heart condition. He likes sleeping sideways with the sofa against his back. I pretty much have one eye open at all times. I watch him. I listen to the sound of his breathing. Audriana usually sleeps down there with me, too. Every once in a while, I'll give her the whole bed and sleep in my own room, but it's a rare treat. I'm just too afraid, with his unstable health, that something could happen.

So anyway, we went to the hospital because he was having trouble breathing, and they took chest X-rays and did other tests. Blah, blah, blah; they did everything. And they saw some fluid in his lungs. Fortunately, the fluid was from the blood that was going down his throat. Thank God, otherwise they said it could have been a sign of pneumonia, which was what my mom had when they first admitted her, and what my dad had around the time she passed. In my father's case, it was presenting more like a sinus infection. The doctor said he'd be fine and that I could go to Italy, but that they wanted to admit him to the ICU. *The ICU? What? Why?* I freaked out at first. How could I leave the country while he was in intensive care? But they reassured me by saying that they just had to keep him overnight to make sure they could get his nose to stop bleeding and so that they could give him antibiotics for the sinus infection and let them kick in.

So my dad was admitted. He wasn't allowed to come home with us.

I called my brother, who came to the hospital. I had to go

home because my girls were home by themselves. But I went right back again the next morning early, since my flight wasn't until that night.

I still wasn't sure if I should go to Milan. It seemed so far away. Too far away. I got in touch with Jim and said, "My father is in the hospital, tell them I can't go to Italy." Believe me, it was not a phone call I wanted to have to make. The show invests a lot of time, energy, and money into planning these trips. I wasn't sure what they were going to say. I mean, I was sure they weren't going to be happy about it, but I had to make certain that my dad was stable, otherwise I wasn't going to go. He was my top priority.

Fortunately, my producer said it wasn't a problem. They totally understood. What else could they say?

By the time 11:00 a.m. rolled around, I was still at the hospital and there was a car scheduled to pick me up and take me to the airport at three o'clock. I still hadn't finished packing! Not to mention that I was so exhausted I could barely keep my eyes open.

I took the doctor aside and said, "Listen, are you absolutely sure he's okay? Please be completely honest with me. Otherwise I'm not going out of town. Do you understand?" My father has known his doctor for about thirty years and we're very close with him, so I knew he'd tell me either "Teresa, you can go" or "Teresa, you can't go." And he said, "Teresa, you should go. He's going to be fine. I'll be here watching him. I'm going to keep him in the ICU for now."

Even though the ICU sounds intimidating, I realized that, if I was going to be out of town, it was the best place for him to be. When he's in intensive care, he gets twenty-four-hour-a-day attention, literally around the clock. That's when I feel safe, because I know if anything happens, there will be doctors and nurses close by to jump in. I also knew that my brother would be home, which gave me peace of mind, especially since I was going to have to put my sixteen-year-old Gia in charge of my other daughters, which I wasn't entirely thrilled about.

My dad ended up staying in the hospital for the entire week, straight through until Friday. Gia's boyfriend took her there after school to visit him, and my kids had to rely on Uber or rides from their friends' parents in order to get to their activities. Thank God the girls and I have great, loyal friends who live nearby. Everybody helped out. I told them that I was working, that I was out of town, and that my father was in the hospital, so people were extremely sympathetic and made sure everything ran as seamlessly as possible in my absence. It wasn't ideal; my friends' generosity was really touching.

The whole time I was away, I called the hospital constantly to see how my dad was doing. They all know me there because my dad is a frequent patient. They gave me all the updates on him. And he has a cell phone, so I could call him directly without a problem. My brother was great, too. He and my father encouraged me to go.

Still, I couldn't help but feel badly for Gia. When I first saw her after I returned from Italy, she had a little breakdown. She started crying, because she was so stressed out from the previous week and having to be responsible for her sisters. She needed me, and I couldn't be there.

Those are the moments when I get really frustrated with Joe and wish that he was here and that he'd never screwed up. I don't want my kids to have to go through this. But once the doctor gave me the okay, I decided I had to go to Italy. It was for work, and these trips are major events on the show. The thing is, it wouldn't have mattered as much if the kids' father had been around to pick up the slack.

Though I do believe the fact that I got to go was meant to be. For me, it was an unbelievable experience, which came at the exact right time in my life—as funny as that may sound. I needed to reconnect with my mother.

So, going back, I did end up making my flight on Monday evening. That was a close call! Of course, people recognized all of us on the plane. The person next to me told me that, even though he'd never actually watched the show, his friend was a huge fan. He was a sweet, cute guy. He said, "Can I take a picture with you?" I said okay, even though I was really hoping he wasn't going to annoy me the whole time. Isn't that the worst? When the passenger sitting with you wants to chat nonstop? I don't like to talk on planes. I like to sleep, especially when I'm going internationally. But, as it turned out, he was really cool. He said, "Do you want me to wake you up when the food comes?" I smiled, and said, "Yes, please!" Then he left me alone and was very respectful. I appreciated that, because I was so tired and spent from the last couple of days.

We took off shortly after six o'clock, and I slept through the entire ride, with just a brief break to eat. I love motion: cars, planes, trains, busses. I'm out like a light right away.

As soon as we arrived in Milan, I went to my room to lie down. I had a beautiful room with a terrace. Melissa was excited to be there so she could buy some European pieces for her clothing store, Envy. Margaret also wanted to shop—she was planning to visit an Italian shoe factory, because she said she wanted to continue to grow her brand as well.

When filming began, our first stop was the Duomo cathedral. I really wanted to go there because my mom loved churches. That was her thing, and it's mine now, too. I feel so connected to her when I'm at church. And since she was born in Italy I knew that being at a church in her home country would connect me to her on a whole different level. My mom was very religious. She loved rosaries and statues of Jesus and Mary, really any saint. She was into all of it. When my mom was alive my parents would go to places like Atlantic City and Pennsylvania with these prayer groups, and they'd carry a statue of Mary with them.

So, starting our trip off at the Duomo was perfect for me. I had a rosary that someone had made me with my mom's photo on it, and I carried that with me everywhere we went.

The next day, I filmed in the Navigli neighborhood, which

is known for the Naviglio Grande and Naviglio Pavese canals. It's one of the most historic districts in Milan, dating back to 1179. There are all these amazing shops and restaurants and fun bars. It's a very cool scene. We walked around there, and there were paparazzi taking our pictures. It was really fun.

Once we wrapped, Dolores and I passed another beautiful church, so we decided to pop in quickly. Dolores is very religious; she appreciates that stuff in the same way I do. I took a video and posted it on Instagram with the caption: *I love you Mommy* #milan

That day Dolores, Margaret, and I also went food shopping and cooked with an Italian chef. That was right up my alley! It was a totally authentic Italian meal. We made homemade pappardelle with a Bolognese sauce. We stuffed zucchini flowers, threw together salad, and assembled carpaccio. When we were making the carpaccio, the chef told me to hit the cutting board really hard. So I did what he said, and I broke it! I guess I must have had some aggression bottled up! Needless to say, the carpaccio was pushed to the side. We took the fractured cutting board as a sign, and avoided the carpaccio at all costs.

But the zucchini and pasta were out of this world. I think they use different flour to make the pasta. It tastes so different than the pasta you eat in America. And we made it without using a machine or anything. We did everything by hand, which was awesome. I'd done it before with my mother and father when I was growing up, but I'd forgotten how challenging it is to make it completely from scratch. First, you have to mix the dough, then you have to roll it out and cut it yourself. It takes a long time. I remembered how my mother used to be so patient with it. It was really sentimental for me. Everything in Italy made me think of my mom. I felt really connected to her there.

The next day I took Siggy to a praying spot with this gorgeous statute of Jesus near this church on an old historic road, off the beaten path, and we ended up praying together in front of the statue. It was very intense.

I prayed to my mother and talked to her. I said the Our Father, because she always said that she loved that prayer. Siggy recited it with me.

> *Our Father, who art in heaven,*
> *hallowed be thy name.*
> *Thy kingdom come.*
> *Thy will be done*
> *on earth as it is in heaven.*
> *Give us this day our daily bread,*
> *and forgive us our trespasses,*
> *as we forgive those who trespass against us;*
> *and lead us not into temptation,*
> *but deliver us from evil. Amen.*

This was something different for Siggy. She's Jewish, so she typically says her prayers in a synagogue, but she didn't care about that. One of the reasons why I love Siggy so much is that, when my mom was in the hospital, she asked Dolores to take her to church with her. She said, "I want to pray for Teresa's mom." That really meant a lot to me. The same way it did to have her there next to me in Italy, in front of the beautiful statue of Jesus.

I was crying a lot and talking to my mom from the heart. I said, "I miss you so much. I think about you all the time. Every minute, every second, every hour of the day. And Gia, Gabriella, Milania, and Audriana miss you. We all miss you. Joey. Daddy. I wish you wouldn't have left me so soon. I used to talk to you ten or fifteen times a day. You were my everything. I'm lost without you. I need your guidance. I need you to show me the way. I think God brought me here to be more connected to you, because I know this is where you were born."

I really felt like that was true. I'd never felt closer to my mother, since she died, than on that trip. I'd been to Milan before. In fact, it was my third time visiting. The last time I'd been there, over a decade earlier, I was five months pregnant with Milania. That's how I got her name. Milan with an "ia" on the end. I'll never forget how we went to Rome after that, and I walked up more than five hundred steps, all the way to the top of the Vatican, with Milania in my belly.

After saying the prayers with Siggy, we had one final dinner at the hotel for the last night of the trip. It was really nice.

Overall, it was one of the best experiences of my lifetime. Just being able to do things like sit outside on the terrace of my hotel room eating breakfast alone was such a treat for me. It's rare that I get peaceful moments like that on a daily basis or ever really. My life is really hectic, so this felt really special and rare to me. It allowed me to meditate and reflect without interruption. I was able to concentrate on me for a change. A lot of the houses and buildings in Italy have balconies, which reminded me of my mom and how she used to do the same thing when she was growing up in her small town. It was bittersweet, feeling at one with her while, at the same time, missing her so much it made my insides ache. That's the thing about loss— you never know when and how it's going to hit you. It just creeps up on you at the strangest times.

I can't entirely explain it, but everything felt different while I was in Milan. I felt lighter, more free, more like myself. Everything is so pure and fresh there, like I was saying with the food. In addition to the pasta, I definitely indulged in plenty of gelato, too! Oh my God, I love, love, love gelato. It's so creamy and delicious, even better than ice cream. My favorite flavors are coffee and pistachio, but don't get me wrong, I'm a big fan of classic chocolate, too. I wish I could have brought a million cartons of it home with me for the kids! You know what's really the best, though? The prosciutto. There's nothing like it. I swear. Again, it's not at all like the prosciutto we eat in the United States. It's not processed in any way. None of the food there is. Everything is so natural. The tomatoes are riper, which makes the sauce better. The fruit is juicier, like it just fell off the tree, which it probably did. *Everything* tastes better in Italy. It really does; I'm not just saying that.

That's what my mom was always trying to re-create when she came to America. She bought everything fresh. That's the way I grew up. I try to do that as often as possible for my own family. It was nice to have that reminder.

It was nice to have all the reminders. Like how the narrow cobblestone streets made me think about when I was in Italy with my mom as a child. In her tiny little town there were no wide paved roads. There were no highways. There were no SUVs. It was not noisy or congested. Although there are plenty of scooters, like Vespas, zipping around which is awesome! I totally want one of those. I could see myself having a house in Italy one day. It's a great escape.

I just allowed myself to soak up all the old-world charm during my time there—from the mouthwatering food and the gorgeous churches with their grand architecture to the quiet, narrow pathways and walking arm in arm with the other House-wives, the same way my mother and father used to. That's how you do it over there. It's like going back in time. Sometimes, I felt like I was on a movie set. It's that breathtaking.

Not to mention all the cute guys! I love their accents and the way they dress. Italians definitely know how to do it better in every way!

Even though Milan is a city and obviously much bigger and more bustling than where my parents were raised, it still re-minded me of them in so many ways. I was able to speak Italian all the time. There's something to be said for communicating in another language. It made me feel very at home. It made me feel like I was where I belonged, even if my mother, father, husband, and daughters couldn't be there with me.

I would say that my journey to Italy felt more like a pilgrimage of sorts, as opposed to a work trip or a vacation. That's why I believe everything happens for a reason.

I was meant to go.

I was destined to be as close to my mother as I could possibly be. To follow her path.

Now I know, more than ever, that she's looking down on me.

15

HOLY DAY, HORRIBLE NIGHT

The day I got back from Italy, my father was released from the hospital, and the next day we had Audriana's First Communion, which is an extremely important tradition in the Catholic faith. It's a ceremony in church where you receive the Eucharist— a Christian rite that is considered a sacrament. The different elements of the Eucharist, bread and wine (or grape juice!), are consecrated and consumed. First Communion, which is typically received when you're around second-grade age, is also the third of seven sacraments: baptism, confirmation, Eucharist, penance, anointing of the sick, holy orders, and matrimony.

The night before the Communion had been pretty intense. I didn't arrive home until around six o'clock in the evening, so I had just enough time to be with the kids and catch up with them before they ran off to meet with friends and I had to work. My good friend Rosana had flown in from California for the Communion and we're also developing a show together—separate from *Real Housewives*—which I'm going to be executive producing. I can't talk about it yet, but it's very exciting! So we ended up meeting, even though I was completely exhausted and jet-lagged. We hung out, had a drink, and worked on the show until really late. Then I went to pick up one of my girls from her friend's house. I didn't get home until about twelve thirty or one o'clock in the morning. But, that's my life. There's very little time for sleep.

The following morning, the day of the Communion, I was up at seven to get my hair done, even though I didn't actually start until around eight because my hairdresser was late, which she always is. I was ready to kill her! Audriana, Milania, and I were all getting our hair done by her, and I still had to have my makeup done, too. Thankfully, Gia and Gabriella were able to do their own hair and makeup. This is how it is when you have a house full of girls! We all love, love, love our glam time.

We had to be at the church by eleven thirty. They had a photographer there to take pictures before everything started at noon. Audriana wore the most stunning white dress, which she designed herself at Little Nikki's boutique in Ho-Ho-Kus, New Jersey. It was sleeveless and had an enormous puffy white skirt with all sorts of embellishments, like flowers and other overlaid designs. There were also a lot of crystals sewn on, including the whole belt around her waist. She had on white satin gloves with more bling at the wrists and a tiara to match her dress, which had a waist-length veil attached to it. She had on a pearl bracelet and her hair was in the sweetest ringlets. She looked beyond gorgeous. Like a Disney princess! I couldn't have been more proud.

I wore cutout white lace pants that had white shorts underneath and a white lace spaghetti strap top by Nicole Miller that I absolutely loved. And we had an amazing cake, which was in the shape of a huge white cross. It had big white flowers on it, edible gold rosary beads with a cross on the end, and piped in gold icing read, "God Bless Audriana 05•13•2017." There were also chocolate and vanilla cupcakes with white icing lined up on either side. I took photos of Audriana standing next to a portrait of my mother. The entire experience reminded me of her and we knew she was looking down on Audriana with the deepest love and pride.

Since Joe wasn't able to be there with us, I didn't want to do anything fancy. It's just too difficult to celebrate in a major way when he's not there to help out. So we kept it low-key and invited immediate family only. It was just me, my daughters, and my dad. Joe's brother came a bit later, though his sister couldn't be there since she was out of town for her birthday. Their kids came, as did my mother-in-law. Unfortunately Joey and Melissa also had to miss out because Melissa's nephew was getting married. Beyond that, it was my friend Rosana and Audriana's godparents. Dina Manzo is her godmother and our friend John is her godfather.

We met John and his family at the beach years ago when Gia and their daughter were only five. They just started playing together and we started talking, and we've remained friends ever since. He's the nicest guy. In fact, we were supposed to go to Puerto Rico with John and his wife and Dina and her boyfriend for New Year's, but I couldn't go because of my mom. The nice thing was that they were all able to go together and ended up becoming close with one another.

Dina is like a sister to me, so when I found out the big news that she and her boyfriend, Dave, had gotten engaged, I was beyond excited! I love, love, love Dave. They've been together for about three years, and he's the greatest guy. They're really cute together. I was dying when she told me. I'm not kidding. I was so happy when I saw that ring on her finger. She wanted to surprise all of us, so she didn't even tell me at first. I just saw this big, shiny rock as she was waving her hand in the air and I thought, "Wow, that's a really gorgeous new piece of jewelry Dina has on. Good for her!" But it didn't register immediately. I was going to ask her, but then I got sidetracked with who knows what. I have four kids. There is *always* something going on. There is *always* someone asking me for something. If I had a penny for every time one of my daughters says, "Mom!" I'd be a zillionaire! So, I swear, I saw the ring, but it didn't dawn on me that Dave had proposed.

But then she pulled me aside and said, "Dave and I got engaged!" And I said, "What? When? How could you have kept that a secret from me?" She said, "A few weeks ago, but I really wanted to wait to tell you in person." I was over the moon for her. You don't understand, I love, love, love Dina. I really, really love her so much. I think she's beautiful inside and out and just the sweetest, most authentic person. All I want is to see her happy. She's been married twice before and it didn't work out either time, so for her to find this fabulous man is truly a gift. Dina always wanted another child—she has one daughter, Lexie, with her first husband—but I feel like she got cheated out of growing a family further, because her second husband, Tommy, didn't want to have any more kids. I mean, I met Dina when she was pregnant with Lexie. She just wanted to be married, be happy, have the big family, and entertain her friends. She has such an amazing sense of style and a truly giving heart. I could not be more thrilled for them.

One might think that her happiness would shine a light on my own difficult situation with Joe, but I'm not petty like that. And that's how much I love her. She's always been supportive of me, through my highest of highs and my lowest of lows. That's what real friends do. Unfortunately, it's taken me more than four decades to realize that. There are people who will pretend they care for you. There are people who will say they take pleasure in your good fortune and want only the best for you. But you have to watch your back. You have to weed out the fake friends.

When I went to prison, I learned who the people I could trust were. I also learned who the people I couldn't trust were. And while my future with Joe may be uncertain at the moment,

I was happy with him. I really was. Until all of this happened. I try to look at this as a bump in the road. When I think about Dina and Dave, it makes me grateful for what I had for so many years. She was married to two guys who treated her like shit. I never had to deal with that. Joe was a pretty good husband until he royally fucked up.

Anyway, it was so wonderful to be with Dina to celebrate her engagement and Audriana's First Communion. It's really special to be able to have loved ones surrounding you for these milestones.

The ceremony was beautiful. All the girls were in white, and the boys were in nice suits. There were about twenty of them and they were so adorable! The priest prayed and called each of them up one at a time to bless them. And then he gave them the Eucharist for them to eat for the first time. It's a very significant rite of passage. Audriana was beaming.

After the church, we went to a restaurant nearby and had dinner. In the past, for my other daughters, I've done something much splashier. I mean, for the kids' christenings, I went completely overboard. They were like weddings! But—again—without Joe, my mother, and my father-in-law, it just didn't feel right.

Actually, Joe's brother ended up making a very touching speech saying how he was sure that Joe would have loved to be with us, but that there were circumstances that didn't allow for that. He also told Audriana how much he loved her and said that he wished his father and my mother could be there with us.

A lot of people were crying, including my dad. So then Audriana got very upset and ran off crying, too. Gia and I went after her to make sure she was okay.

All she could say was that she wished her nonna, her grandfather, and her father could be there. It's not a walk in the park for any of us. Yet when you're only seven years old and it's an important day for you, it's even harder. Especially because she's still too young to truly understand why her mother had to leave her for almost a year, and then her father had to go, too. We all try to stay strong. But, on certain occasions that's easier said than done. And there's nothing I can say that will make it better.

Still, despite Audriana being distraught about her father and grandparents, everyone came back to our house and celebrated some more. We sat around drinking and eating cheese and sausage until late into the evening. I don't know why I even bother hosting events at restaurants! Everyone always comes back to my house anyway. But I didn't care, because Audriana told me that it was the best day ever, which made me so happy to hear. All I want is for my daughters to be happy and healthy.

Unfortunately, what I didn't know is that the night would end in tragedy. Shortly before eleven, after leaving my house about an hour earlier, Dina and her fiancé, Dave, returned to their town house in Holmdel, New Jersey, to find two masked assailants inside. When they opened the door, the guys rushed at them and attacked them. One of them hit Dave a bunch of times with a baseball bat, resulting in a broken nose, and the other punched Dina multiple times, resulting in facial injuries. Then the creeps tied them up and stole cash and jewelry before fleeing the scene. Fortunately, Dave was able to free himself and call the police. I hope they catch those fuckers. *They* are criminals.

Dina and Dave live in Malibu but rent the place in Holmdel because Dave's kids from his first marriage still live in New Jersey. They'd flown into town just to be there for Audriana's Communion. I don't even know how anyone found out that they'd be in New Jersey. We didn't publicize the Communion or even post anything about it on social media until after the fact. I was in total shock when I found out, which wasn't until Sunday night—twenty-four hours later—and even then I didn't believe it. I got a call from one of my friends—not one of the cast or former cast members—who said, "Somebody broke into a New Jersey Housewife's home." I said, "What are you talking about?" And she said, "In Holmdel, New Jersey. I just heard something about it on the news." I said, "That doesn't make any sense. None of the Housewives live in Holmdel." So I didn't think anything of it. Dave's ex-wife and kids live in Colts Neck, New Jersey, which is about ten minutes away from Holmdel, but I still didn't put two and two together. I didn't even know they were renting a town house there or where exactly they were staying that night. It never, ever occurred to me that it could be Dina, especially since she was no longer a Housewife.

The following morning, Monday, my lawyer, Jim, called

me first thing and told me exactly what had happened. I freaked out! I mean, I literally went crazy. All I could think about was how she'd just told me that she and Dave were engaged and how happy they'd looked at Audriana's Communion. I knew that she was planning to be with her mom on Mother's Day— the day after the Communion—and that she was going to tell her the amazing news then. That's why I didn't talk to her on Sunday. I felt like she was going to have that special time with her mom, and I wanted to give her the space she deserved. And then I knew she had reservations to fly back to Malibu on Monday. I just figured we'd catch up about her upcoming wedding and other details when she got home.

When I heard from Jim, I was so heartbroken. I called Dina immediately, but she didn't answer. Then I called Dave, and he didn't answer, either, so I left a message saying, "Call me!" I was frantic. Thank God he called me right back and explained exactly what had happened. I said, "Is it true?" And he said, "Unfortunately, yes." He told me they'd been tied up, that Dina had been punched in the face, and that he'd been hit over the head with a baseball bat. He said they had no warning. The guys were there waiting for them when they got home. It was a very quick conversation because his lawyer was beeping through on the other line and he had to speak to him. I was just so relieved to hear his voice.

A little while after I spoke to Dave, Dina called me. She was still in the hospital and was hysterical. She was crying so hard. She just kept saying, "I got punched." I felt devastated for her.

I said, "I am so, so sorry. I love you." I would have visited her in the hospital if there was time, but they were released right after that, and they took the first flight back to California. They wanted to recover in the comfort of their own home. Who could blame them? Malibu is very healing for her. She loves living there and being removed from all the drama in New Jersey. I swear to you, if I hadn't been in the midst of filming the final episodes of the next season, I'd have been out there with her. I felt so awful that I couldn't go there immediately and help take care of her. She's been such a good friend to me and it was frustrating that I couldn't take the time to be there for her in person. Fortunately, Dina's daughter flew out to see her. I texted Dina and she texted me back saying she was doing okay, all things considered. Then I texted Dave and said, "I love you guys. Just checking in." He texted me back, "We love you too." That made me feel a little bit better.

I told Dina that since summer is so short here, I'll visit her in the fall. I want to go out there for a week in September and take the kids out of school when they have a couple of days off.

The scary thing is that what happened to Dina and Dave could happen to anyone. I mean, is anyone really safe? Am I safe? Are my kids safe? When I told Joe what had happened, he was devastated, too. He's known Dina for a long time, and he's always loved her. He said he wants me to get an even better security system than the one we have. And he's absolutely right. We have a big gate and a stone wall and an alarm, but my house isn't a fortress. It's not Fort Knox. These crooks are smart, and if they can break into other people's homes, banks, jewelry stores, and things like that, who knows if they could break into my house? It's terrifying to think of when I have four young daughters and my elderly father living with me. I'm responsible for all of them. Not to mention that I'm on television, which makes me a target.

Ever since Dina's break-in, I've felt very nervous and jittery. Dina told me that she's scared now. She doesn't want to be afraid, but how can she not be? Someone violated her space and then attacked her physically. There's no way to forget that. She's walking on eggshells. She's looking around every corner. She's aware of who's in front of her, who's next to her, and who's behind her. When something like this happens, suddenly you feel like people are following you or out to get you. You lose faith and trust in everything you thought you knew. Even though, thank God, I didn't go through what Dina did, I can understand that on some level. She doesn't know who she can depend on.

With Joe gone for three years, I do get scared in the house sometimes. I do worry about what would happen if someone tried to get to me or, even worse, my daughters. That's what husbands are for! To make you feel secure. But, listen, Dave was with Dina, and there was nothing he could do to save either of them. The terrifying thing is that these criminals carry guns and knives and baseball bats! They don't care if they hurt you, because all they want is money and loot. I mean, why couldn't they have just tied them up and robbed them? Why did they have to inflict bodily harm? It seems so unnecessary.

It's horrible to even think about, but I have no choice because I'm the only person in charge of keeping my family safe while Joe's away. And that's a big burden to bear.

My heart goes out to Dina and Dave and all their loved ones. What happened to my friends was an unspeakable tragedy that I will never forget. I only thank God that they're okay. It could have been so much worse.

I know she's going to get through this. Dina has always been there for me, and now I'll do the same for her. Healing doesn't happen overnight, but she will get there. And I'll do everything in my power to help her mend.

___

16

HONORING MOM

*M*other's Day 2017 did not start out happy for me, my brother, or my father. Joey said he woke up crying, whereas my dad and I didn't want to think about it at all. It had been just two short months since my mom left us, and we still felt so raw. There's really no way to explain how that kind of loss takes over your life. You want to move on, yet at the same time you don't, because you don't want to forget the sound of the person's voice or the expressions they made. You don't want to forget how their skin felt or even how they smelled. There are so many things you take for granted when your loved ones are still alive. Like the fact that I used to be able pick up the phone at any hour of any day and call my mother about anything— from a funny story about the kids I wanted to tell her to a bigger problem I was having with work or with Joe. She was my sounding board.

Most days, there's so much going on and life is so hectic, that it's easier not to dwell on it. But when there's a holiday devoted entirely to a celebration of motherhood, it's impossible not to think about her.

Don't get me wrong, I love thinking about my mother and remembering her and how wonderful she was. Sometimes, I'll sit and look back at recent photos of her with me, my dad, and the girls, or even older pictures of me and Joey from childhood. My mom was so beautiful and full of love that it gives me strength. She was the best role model I could have ever asked for. I strive to be the kind of mother to my kids that my mom was to me, and I hope that my daughters feel like they can look up to and count on me the way I did with my mom. I hope they call me a million times a day when they grow up. A strong mother-daughter relationship is truly a gift.

Even though my mother is no longer here on earth with us, I know she's still looking down on us and guiding us. I feel her presence and talk to her all the time.

While I wasn't as excited to celebrate Mother's Day for myself this year, I knew it was important to the kids. That's why I kept my emotions about my mom at bay and pushed through for my daughters. That's what a good mom does—she puts her children first—as my mom always did.

So I got up bright and early to go pick up Gabriella at seven thirty from a sleepover she'd had at a friend's house, because my father wanted to go to the cemetery to visit my mom at eight sharp. He also wanted to go out and buy me flowers, which he and Gabriella did together as soon as she got home. I thought that was so cute and sweet! Poor kid was exhausted because she'd stayed up really late with her friend and had then woken up very early to come home to be with me. That's what my kids are like. Really thoughtful and heartfelt.

When they gave me the flowers I was so taken aback. I said, "Oh my God! You didn't have to get me anything!" I guess I didn't expect it because I wasn't in the mood to celebrate and I didn't want to upset my dad. Once my dad gets going on my mom, he really works himself up and, with his touch-and-go health, I don't need him getting worked up! But my dad was able to put his feelings about my mom aside and focus on the fact that it was still Mother's Day for me and for his grand-daughters, which I thought was amazing. He's the best father and nonno in the whole wide world! After that he went to visit his sister to wish her a happy Mother's Day, too. Like my mother, my dad is a very selfless and compassionate person. I try to teach those values to my girls.

Once my dad got home from his sister's house, Audriana was so excited about her Holy Communion the day before that she said, "I can't wait to have the host again!" The host is the consecration of the bread. And the bread and wine symbolize the separation of Jesus's body from his blood at Calvary. Basically, she wanted to go right back to church again, which I thought was so beautiful. So I said, "Okay, let's go!"

Around twelve o'clock Gia, Gabriella, Milania, Audriana, my father, and I went to church. I got very emotional while we were there because they sang the Ave Maria, which is what they sang at my mom's church on the day of her funeral. They had this unbelievably talented singer, who sounded like she could be in the opera. Her voice was incredible, and I just lost it. I couldn't stop thinking about my mom. Everything I'd been bottling up from Audriana's Communion the day before and all morning just came rushing out. At one point, Audriana looked at me and said, "Mommy, are you crying?" And then she gave me a hug. My dad was crying, too. I could see him wiping his tears, even though he wasn't sitting next to me. I didn't want to look at him, because I knew that would make it harder for both of us.

After church, we all went to the cemetery, because only my dad and Gabriella had gone in the morning. You can't bring fresh flowers to a mausoleum, so instead I brought Audriana's Communion photo. It was a card with her picture on it, and then when you opened it up, the menu from the restaurant we ate at that night was inside. I wanted my mom to see that. So we left it for her on the table right by where she's buried.

Once we'd all wished my mom a happy Mother's Day, we came home and had our Italian dinner as we always do on Sundays. My father had gotten up really early to make the sauce, which he'd put beef and oxtail bones in for flavor. We also had salad, meatballs, cavatelli, and braciole, which is meat rolled up with parsley and garlic. It's so delicious!

Gia gave me a gorgeous Swarovski crystal case for my

cell phone, and the younger girls always make stuff for me at school. Milania bought me a beautiful plant, which we planted outside in our garden. Gabriella wrote me this beautiful note, which had me bawling when I read it:

> *Happy Mother's Day to the most strongest woman I know out there. I've grown up to be the great kid you've raised me to be. You mean the world to me even if I don't appreciate it sometimes but I want you to know that I'm so grateful to have the best mother in the world. I wouldn't be where I am in life without the help of you. You're an inspiration to me in every which way possible.* ❤❤*XOXOX*

And Audriana did this spectacular project, where she took every letter of the alphabet and wrote something about me with all sorts of different colors and drawings of flowers, hearts, and rainbows. I couldn't believe how amazing it was and how much thought went into it. It must have taken her forever! She's only seven! Here are a few of the letters.

A is for always
You always make me feel better and be kind and respectful. And you always be nice to me.

B is for beautiful
You are beautiful because your hair is always pretty and your face is so pretty and you always have pretty clothes.

C is for caring

You show you care about me when I fall or if I cry you'll always help me and you are so nice and kind.

D is for dear

You are dear to me because you are never mean to me

E is for encourage

You always encourage me to do good on my competitions and gymnastics

F is for fun

We have fun together when we have mommy and daughter day and when we get ice cream.

G is for grateful

I am grateful for you because you're the best mom ever and if another person was my mom I would run to your house and give you a big hug. Mommy you're as sweet as candy!!!

T is for tough

Sometimes I have to do hard things and you help me through. Something tough you have helped me with is my homework and taking me to dance and gymnastics.

U is for understand

Whenever I have a problem I know you will understand.
I appreciate you when you help me and when you never
yell at me and when you don't yell at my sisters.

V is for very

You are very important to me because I always want you
to be on my side and you are the best mom in the world.

W is for wish

You are so special to me. If I had one wish for you I
would want you to never go on vacation because I can't
take it because I'm too far from you.

X is for xoxo

Hugs and kisses I send your way.

Y is for years

Many more years that I want to spend with you.

Z is for a zillion

A zillion times you have shown your love to me.

And that wasn't all! She also crafted three colorful "cell
phones" out of paper. She made up questions that I would ask
her and then wrote in the answers that she would give. She

made it look like text messages between us. It was so creative!
Here's what they said:

Hi, sweetie!
Hi Mom I LOVE U

Do you know what my real name is?
Yes Teresa

How old do you think I am?
36

How much do you think I weigh?
100 something

If we could spend one whole day together, what would
we do?
Mommy and daughter

What am I as pretty as?
A flower

What wouldn't you trade me for?
All the fidget spinners in the world.

What is my favorite color?
Green

What is my favorite place to shop?
Robyn's Closet

What am I the best at making?
Pasta

Of course I especially enjoyed the fact that she said I'm thirty-six! That's my girl! Oh, and the fact that she wouldn't trade me for all the fidget spinners in the world is hysterical.

When all was said and done, even though I didn't think it was going to be the happiest day—with my mother gone and my husband gone in a different way—it ended up being great.

I guess the moral here is that family is the most important thing. It's what I revolve my life around. And when I'm surrounded by those who are closest to me, there isn't an obstacle or a tragedy that's insurmountable.

AVE MARIA

Ave Maria
Ave Maria
Vergin del ciel
Virgin of the sky
Sovrana di grazie e madre pia
Sovereign of thanksgiving and loving mother
Accogli ognor la fervente preghiera
Accept the fervent prayer of everybody

Non negar

Do not refuse

A questo smarrito mio amor

To this lost person of mine, love

Tregua nel suo dolor!

Truce in his pain!

Sperduta l'alma mia ricorre a te

My lost soul turns to you

E piena di speme si prostra ai tuoi pie

And full of repentment, humbles at your feet

T'invoca e attende la vera pace

It invokes you and waits for the true peace

che solo tu puoi donar

that only you can give

Ave Maria

Ave Maria

Ave Maria, gratia plena,

Ave Maria, full of thanksgiving

Maria, gratia plena

Maria, full of thanksgiving

Maria, gratia plena

Maria, full of thanksgiving

Ave Ave Dominus

Ave Ave God

Dominus tecum

Your God

Benedicta tu in mulieribus,

Be blessed among the women,
et benedictus
and blessed
et benedictus fructus ventris
and blessed be the product of your womb
ventris tui, Iesus.
your womb, Jesus.
Ave Maria
Ave Maria

17

ANOTHER BIRTHDAY,
A NEW VENTURE,
AND A VISIT TO PRISON

*W*hen I woke up on the morning of my forty-fifth birthday—just four days after Mother's Day—I was not happy. Even though I felt so much younger than my age, I still hated getting older. What woman doesn't?

Not to mention that it made me think about my mom and how she was taken away from us at such a young age. It's so unfair.

I'm not typically too enthusiastic about my birthday anyway, but with Joe and my mother not there, I was even more bummed out than usual.

What I also found out that day was that my luggage had been broken into on our way home from Italy. I didn't notice until I started unpacking that someone had stolen my favorite Chanel shoes and a gorgeous silver Yves Saint Laurent bag that was very expensive. How fucked-up is that? The next time I travel I'm not taking anything nice! I'm bringing cheap shoes. I don't care. It's bullshit! Of course I know it's only stuff, but it still pissed me off. The last thing I needed was to have someone rifle through my bags—even though I have no idea who did it.

On top of that I had to pay a visit to my probation officer. Doesn't that sound like a fantastic gift?

But before that I had to get my kids off to their various schools and go through our whole morning routine. The girls were excited for me, which was nice. They all said, "Happy Birthday, Mom!" and gave me hugs and kisses. That I love, love, love, especially when I'm feeling down. There's nothing in the world that can brighten my spirits faster than my daughters. It's amazing how strong they are. It hasn't been an easy couple of years for any of us, and they always find a way to push through.

Once the kids were off, I fought through rush-hour traffic to meet my lawyer, Jim, in Newark. There was also a graduation going on, so it took me an hour to find a parking spot. I hate that! I was so annoyed and frustrated. I mean, who the hell wants to go see their probation officer on their birthday? Not me. But I had no choice because, unfortunately, I got two traffic tickets. And whenever you have an encounter of any kind with the law, you have to report it. I'd told Jim about them, but when the tickets never came in the mail, we didn't think there was anything to report. We were wrong.

I'd gotten one of the tickets when I was in New York City the previous September heading to the American Girl store to celebrate Audriana's seventh birthday. I was in the right lane, so I could turn right, but I didn't realize you weren't supposed to turn right from there. There are so many rules and regulations in Manhattan that I'm not familiar with. I really didn't know. I swear. It was a total mistake, but it was still stupid. The cop was literally standing on the street and just pointed at me to pull over. I was shocked because I had no idea that I'd done anything bad. It seems like that's always how it is for me.

The other time, I was in New Jersey, and I had my cell phone in my hand while driving. I wasn't even using it, so I don't know why I was just holding it! I was with my father, so I can assure you I wasn't texting or speaking to anyone. My dad doesn't go for that crap. He thinks it's ridiculous that people are even allowed to talk on the phone in the car, namely the driver. He's very old-fashioned that way, which is good, because I want my daughters to learn that safety is important above anything else. Whatever you have to tell someone can wait until you get where you're going!

So, anyway, I got pulled over. Twice. I don't know if the cops recognized me either time. I think some do and some don't, but I never say anything like, "I'm famous." Or, "I'm on television." I know there are actors who've done that sort of stuff and it didn't go well for them. I don't need any more trouble!

As soon as we got in to see my probation officer, it was a pretty easy experience. It was just a two-second thing. Thank

God. All I had to do was sign a piece of paper and then he reminded me of the rules, which I thought I already knew. He said, "Next time call." And I said, "Okay, I will." I'm all about doing everything right, now. I'll be so happy to finally be done with probation on February 4, 2018. Most other people who are incarcerated for a similar crime get a year, but I got two years, which means I've had to stay in the United States if I want to travel. That's why we went to Puerto Rico for vacation.

Fortunately, I did get permission to leave the country to go to Italy because it was for work, so that was fine. You can do anything for work. They just want to make sure you don't flee the country, which isn't an issue for me. Where am I going to go? I have four kids, an ailing father, and a husband in prison! I'm definitely not a flight risk. *Madonna mia!*

Still, being forced to see my probation officer on my birthday just made me think harder about the future—for me and for my kids. We've come through so much and we're so much stronger for it. I really do hope we've put the worst behind us. The kids are doing so well. They're more independent than they ever were before—that's for sure. And they're definitely more empathetic and sympathetic human beings, too. I think sometimes it takes enduring your own stuff to extract you from the ideal world you were living in. Or the ideal world you *thought* you were living in. It allows you to realize that everyone has their shit, and a lot of it is even crappier than yours. Ya know? Obviously I'd never wish our struggles on anyone— adults or children—but those struggles have changed both me and my girls for the better in many ways. That's not to say they didn't have to handle some horrible things, you understand? I'm just making the point that we've been able to learn from the past and now we're looking toward the future as a result of what's happened. The kids are more responsible. They don't take as much for granted as they used to, which is huge, because it's easy to get spoiled when you have everything on demand. Believe me, I know. And they also recognize that life isn't perfect. They know that people can go through difficult times and come out okay—maybe even better for it. They all want to pay it forward in life, which is pretty amazing when you think about what the alternative could have been.

I'm just relieved to finally feel like a lot of the negative is behind us. That said, while we have been to hell and back, I don't know that I'll feel completely settled until Joe gets home and is situated in his own life and career. That's when I'll feel like I can really relax and be totally positive about everything. But I try not to think about that. I put all of my efforts into focusing on the good things that are happening for all of us. The girls are excelling in everything that they do. And I'm finally at a point where I can turn my efforts toward growing a lifestyle brand for myself.

As I said, I'm determined to build a Teresa Giudice empire. I know I can do it if I put my mind to it. I'm starting to make inroads into creating lines of shoes, clothing, exercise gear, and accessories. Also bathing suits and cover-ups. I love, love, love swimwear so that would be perfect for me. Everyone keeps telling me I should do a children's line, too. I'm really into that, because I shop with my four daughters constantly. If there's anyone who knows kids' apparel, it's me, for sure! I'd also love to branch out into things for the home, such as decor and whatnot. That's what's on the horizon for me. I want to be the next Martha Stewart. Margaret Josephs said she'd introduce me to the right people, since her company does a lot of the same stuff I'm hoping to do. I'm really looking forward to that. There are so many avenues to pursue, and I'm beyond ready and motivated.

I'm telling you, this is going to be huge for me. I just want to keep working. That's my thing now. I want to keep going and doing more and more and more. I see myself starting a number of businesses. But I'm going to be smarter about it than I have with things in the past. If I decide to partner with someone, for example, I'm going to make sure that they're the right partner. If there's one thing I've learned it's that you always have to dot all your i's and cross all your t's, especially when it comes to your career. You have to be thorough and aware. Your eyes always have to be open. I used to trust everyone, but I know I can't do that anymore. That's how you get taken advantage of.

I also want to write more books, maybe even a lifestyle book, because I love entertaining and everything that goes into that. I like decorating the house for special occasions and holidays, and I love doing a gorgeous table in different colors and themes—with china and nice silverware. It comes naturally to me. It's like breathing. And there's nothing I enjoy more than

playing hostess. That's how I grew up. We always had people over. We had an open-door policy with friends and family
to come over and eat and drink with us. That's still how we
live our lives. The kids always invite friends over, and so do
I. The more the merrier! My parents taught me that, and now
I've passed that on to my own girls. And obviously I also inherited my passion for amazing food and cooking from my mother
and father. It's part of who I am. Listen, I didn't grow up with
a lot of money, but we always had good food on the table and
everybody gathered around. That was a top priority ahead of
fancy things. So I can definitely see incorporating all that into
my brand moving forward. In order to be authentic and to get
people to invest in you, I believe you have to have a true passion for what you're doing and have the true life experience to
back it up. Otherwise people will realize that you're a fraud,
which I'm definitely not. I'm as real as they come!

That's why I'm so, so excited about a brand-new restaurant
that my brother and our family launched in East Hanover, New
Jersey, called Gorga's Homemade Pasta & Pizza. Right after
I met with my probation officer, I went home and started getting ready for the grand opening with my glam squad. This is a
snippet from a piece that ran on nj.com about the restaurant. I
thought the first line was really funny!

On "Real Housewives of New Jersey," star Joe Gorga
has certain, shall we say, retrograde notions of a
woman's place (the kitchen). But that apparently doesn't

extend to business, because he's the man behind a new Italian restaurant that has opened in East Hanover.

Gorga's Homemade Pasta & Pizza is at 360 Route 10 West in East Hanover, and, according to an online job posting for [the] restaurant, it will "specialize in bringing the delicious versions of our family's favorite Italian dishes to you."

I don't know why it didn't mention that our whole family is involved. I mean, Joey does own it, but all of us are pitching in to help out. What's so special is that it's a tribute to our late mom. My brother told *People* magazine, "My mother loved to cook; it was like her drug. I always told her I was gonna open up a restaurant for her. Then I got busy. While I signed a contract on this place we lost her. So this is for her." That made me want to cry. We loved her so much, and she would have been so proud of the restaurant and the fact that it's something that brings us all closer together. She was all about family, family, family. That's why it really hurt her when Joey and I were fighting. She liked it when everyone was getting along and really tight-knit, which we are now. Thank God!

Anyway, the menu is full of really fresh Italian dishes that my mom used to make—everything from scratch. We want to share her food with the world. Some of the dishes are named after family members, which is really cool. There's "Nonna's Meatballs," "Papa's Baked Mussels," "Melissa's Harvest Salad," "Joey's Chopped Salad," "Audriana's Rock Shrimp

Arrabiata," "Antonia's Chicken Francese," and "Gia's Chicken Milanese," among others. A few of the recipes are even in my cookbook *Fabulicious*. We're also selling jars of our homemade pasta sauce—marinara, vodka, and garlic oil—there and on our website. It's so delicious! I use it every Sunday for our Italian dinners at home.

The opening was a huge success, which was awesome! It was so crowded. We were supposed to get tents outside, because the restaurant space is very small, but it didn't work out and it didn't matter. We didn't even need them. We served homemade pasta, which we were making right then and there. It really was such a fun party. I wore an amazing red lace, spaghetti strap dress by Stylestalker. I loved the way I looked and felt that night. Sexy and pretty all in one. We were filming for the show, too. *Extra* came, so we did a scene with them. It ended up being a ninety-degree day, but, thankfully, we had air-conditioning. Everybody said the food was so yummy and that they had the best time. It's officially open for business now, so I hope people come and visit us! I promise it's worth it—you will not be disappointed.

And, if this restaurant does really well, which it will, because I always try to think positive thoughts, then the next one will be even larger. I would love to open them up nationwide—possibly in Las Vegas and Los Angeles to start. Then, who knows? Maybe we'll launch them overseas eventually. I like to think big! That's how my mind works.

I think Joey would like to do that, too. Right now what he

does for work is very stressful. He buys apartment buildings and fixes them up. That's what my husband used to do, so I know that there are so many deadlines and there's so much pressure. I could see him leaving the construction business to own and oversee a bunch of restaurants one day. Melissa is supportive of the restaurant, but it's not her thing. She likes running her clothing shop, Envy, which I believe is going pretty well. Honestly, I don't really shop there that much because the storefront is out of the way for me.

I'd be thrilled to be involved in the restaurants, though! When *Housewives* comes to an end, I could totally see doing that instead. Why not? As I said, I love food and I love to cook. I'm hoping this venture will be lucrative for all of us. Fingers crossed!

Before Joe left for prison, the two of us were planning to buy a restaurant in Morristown, New Jersey. We went to go look at it and everything, but the thing was, we were going to do it with Rino Aprea, who used to be on the show. He and my husband are very close, and he's already in the restaurant business, so Joe wanted to learn everything from him. When you open a restaurant, you often do it with a partner, because it's a tremendous amount of work. Unfortunately, Rino thought it was too much to take on, especially with Joe going away for so long. Also, the property was very expensive.

But back to my birthday . . .

After the opening, I went up the street with a few girlfriends to have a drink. It was late, so we just sat around and talked. To be honest, I wasn't really into it. The only way I can explain it is that it takes a lot for me to have fun these days. It's hard for me to let loose, because I have so many personal issues to deal with. And I just have too much on my mind right now, which makes it difficult to relax. I know once everything is settled, then I'll feel more comfortable having a good time.

I did celebrate with my family the day before, so that was pretty nice. My dad made pasta for dinner and steak pizzaiola, which is my absolute favorite. It was me, my dad, and my kids. Joey and Melissa came over a bit later, too. Melissa got me the ugliest zebra print cake. I was like, "You're kidding me, right? I put you in charge of this one thing and this is what you get?" Then she joked, "You, me, and desserts just don't go good together," in reference to the sprinkle-cookie incident. I don't know. Usually she's got great style, just not when it comes to something for me. She didn't get me a gift, either. Whatever! I got plenty of stuff from my friends.

Siggy gave me a Louis Vuitton scarf, which I thought was so sweet of her. Margaret got me two pairs of exercise leggings. And Danielle said she had something for me, too. As far as my other friends, one got me a candle, one got me flowers, and one got me Prosecco. They know me so well!

The Saturday night after my birthday was Siggy's fiftieth. I took my dad with me as my date. I wore a silver sparkly Herve Leger bandage dress, which was gorgeous. Everyone was told to wear white, black, or silver. Siggy looked so beautiful in a shimmery silver dress with fringes at the bottom. She definitely does not look fifty years old!

It was only me and Dolores from the cast, and my friends Lisa G. and Lisa F. came, too. Siggy met them through me and now they're friends, which I love. The event was held at the Coliseum in White Plains, New York. We snacked on appetizers, sipped cocktails, and there was a DJ, so we danced all night. The space was pretty big, so it didn't seem jammed, which was perfect for me. I don't like a big crowd. The only negative thing was that there were a lot of speeches. I kept thinking, *Oh my God, how many fucking people are going to say something?* I think at events like that you have to keep the speeches to a minimum and, if you are going to get up and say something, you should try to keep it brief. But there are a lot of people who love Siggy and they wanted to tell her (and everyone else!).

Even though I wasn't in the mood to party and I wanted to get home to my kids, I went for a few hours because I adore Siggy. I had as good of a time as I could. Again, because I have a lot going on, my mind is always spinning. It's hard for me to focus on having fun. I like everything to be perfect.

But, it isn't. At least not yet. Even when I'm out at an event or a celebration, like Siggy's, I can't stop thinking about how I have to pay taxes. And how all I want is a clean slate. I feel like people don't get that about me. There's a constant pit in my stomach when things are unsettled. Don't get me wrong, I try to put on a happy face every day, but it takes a lot for me to really let my hair down. Also, I'm not a big drinker. I certainly didn't want to get drunk. That's not my style.

Plus, I knew that the next day I was going to visit Joe and I wanted my head to be as clear as possible for that. At this point, he'd already been in jail for fourteen months, which was longer than the whole time I was there, and he had a couple of more years to go, which was hard to believe. There was still so much I had to deal with and figure out with him gone. I hadn't seen him in a number of those months and his birthday was two days away (the day after I was going to see him), so I knew I needed to do it. The show filmed us driving there. Milania and Audriana came in the car with me. Gabriella had a soccer game, so she couldn't go. And Gia went with my brother because she didn't feel like being filmed, which is understandable. It was also the first time that Joey was going to visit Joe, so she wanted to ride with him. Melissa didn't come. I'm pretty sure she hasn't filled out her paperwork to get permission. I'm also pretty sure that Joe doesn't give a shit. He has a huge family, so he really doesn't need to see her anyway. And, believe me, Melissa would *not* be able to tolerate prison, even if she was just in there for an hour!

To tell you the truth, I was actually a little bit excited to visit Joe, despite the fact that returning to prison brings back so many negative memories of my time there. Even though I'm pissed as hell, I do still miss him at times. I think that's natural. He is my husband after all. Supposedly for better or for worse, right?

We pulled up to the entrance, and I actually felt nervous! In part because of the undesirable memories but also because I truly couldn't wait to see him—even I was a little surprised by that. After we went inside, they brought us to the room where you sit with the inmates, and I was so happy to see Joe. I kissed him, and the girls ran up and kissed him and hugged him. It's complicated because Audriana doesn't entirely understand what's going on, but she was just so thrilled to see her father that she didn't care. Oh, the innocence of youth!

I was shocked by how much Joe had changed! And let me tell you, he looked so friggin' good. He got this side comb-over haircut that I'd told him to get, because I'm very into hair. He just looked really, really hot. I even emailed him after to say, "I can't wait for you to be in my bed again," which he obviously liked hearing. His body is so hard—Oh My God! He's lost so much weight. Too bad there aren't conjugal visits! I really can't wait for him to come home, if only for that reason. Regardless of how I feel, a girl still has needs! And, regardless of what the tabloids are saying, I am *not* cheating on my husband. I never have. Not once. And I never will.

Another thing that happened—and this was where he'd changed beyond just his physical appearance—was he told me that he was sorry. We talked about it while I was there and I said, "You always blame everybody else. You've never really said it was your fault and that you're sorry about what actually happened and everything that came after that." And he replied, "Teresa, I took responsibility. I've been writing emails telling

you how sorry I am. But you're right. I've never said it directly
to your face, which I should have." I really appreciated that,
even though it doesn't fix what happened. It took a lot for him
to go there, and to have that acknowledgment with him looking
into my eyes felt real. For the first time.

He even admitted it to Gia, Milania, and Audriana, which
was most important to me, even if the younger two didn't completely get it. He said, "Yeah, I should've been on top of things
more and I wasn't. I'll never let that happen again. I promise."
That made me feel a little bit better about everything. I told
him in no uncertain terms that when he comes home he has
to be aware of what's going on with our finances. He has to
read every piece of paper that his accountant gives him with a
friggin' magnifying glass. And, no matter what, he has to pay
all our taxes on time. I said, "I don't want any of that shit to
ever happen again. I plan to read every single thing you put in
front of me with a fine-toothed comb. You understand?" He
may look amazing, but that doesn't change the way I feel about
what he did to us.

Listen, no matter how you slice it, prison is a nightmare—for
the person who's in there and for all the family members left
behind. Even though Joe's at a minimum-security facility, it's
still awful. When we visit, there are a lot of people around. You
have to go sit in this big room—it's a lot more spacious than the
one where I was—and there are a lot of other inmates with their
families. People recognize me and say hello to me, but you're not
really supposed to talk to other people's families, so that's tricky

to navigate. It was the same when I was away. I don't like to talk to anybody else anyway—it's uncomfortable and awkward. So, you just sit there and chat. And you can hug and kiss, although I'm not really into too many public displays of affection. The kids, however, were all over Joe. They were literally hanging on him like he was a tree. It was nice to see that. No matter how I feel about Joe, I want the girls to feel good about him, which they do. I don't want them to hold any resentment in their hearts toward him. That's extremely important to me, because I know he never meant to hurt them. That's the last thing he would ever want to do. The girls are everything to him. They were really happy to see their father. And they were even happier that he told them *he'd* made a mistake—not Mommy—and that it would never, ever happen again.

That was so significant, because Gia once made a comment to me like, "Why'd you sign the papers?" And I said, "Why'd I sign them? Because that's what you do. You sign things that your husband gives you. You trust your husband." That's exactly what I did, and I learned the hard way. I think she gets it now.

The funny thing is that the girls think Joe can do no wrong. I mean, granted, he didn't kill someone or rob a bank, but his actions still weren't right. After we left, they all said, "We don't care what he did. We just know that we love him. He's our dad," which is exactly the way it should be. They didn't even cry, even though I did when we were talking about my mom. Joe was saying, "I can't believe your mom isn't here anymore." Then he started crying, and I started crying, too, and he hugged me, because I know he loved my mom so much. It sucks. I could tear up at any moment just thinking about it.

The girls were very excited to wish Joe a happy birthday, especially Milania—they're so close; it's very sweet to watch. The next day she posted this message on her Instagram with a stunning photo of her and Joe dressed in all white on the beach:

OMG HAPPY BIRTHDAY TO YOU, HAPPY BIRTHDAY TO YOU, HAPPY BIRTHDAY DEAR DADDY HAPPY BIRTHDAY TO YOU! I LOVE YOU SO MUCH!! YOU ARE THE BEST DAD EVER! YOU ARE SO AMAZING! YOU ARE SO CARING, NICE, AMAZING AND THE MOST GREATEST DAD EVER! DAD YOU TEACH ME HOW TO DO EVERYTHING! YOU WILL NEVER KNOW HOW MUCH I LOVE YOU! EVEN THOUGH I AM A PAIN IN THE BUTT I STILL LOVE YOU TO THE MOON AND BACK! YOU REALLY CANT EXPLAIN HOW MUCH I CARE AND LOVE YOU! YOU HAVE A SPECIAL PLACE IN MY HEART! I LOVE YOU WITH ALL MY HEART HAPPY BIRTHDAY DADDY!

Gia also posted a picture of her and Joe with the caption:

happy birthday daddy love and miss you so much can't wait for you to make me endlessly laugh everyday xoxo

It was really nice to see Joey and Joe together, too. They have a pretty good relationship now, which makes me happy. My brother cracks me up. When he first saw Joe, because he hadn't seen him in over a year (I could cry about that, too, since they were once so close), he kept saying, "You look so pretty! You look so pretty!" I swear Joe looks thirty years old. It's amazing what being in prison can do for your physical appearance.

I mean, listen, I wish none of this would have happened. It's been a fucking nightmare. But Joe may never have had the opportunity to turn his life around otherwise. This was his wake-up call. He had hit rock bottom with all the financial troubles and then the excessive drinking. We all did. Obviously I wish this would've happened when the kids were younger, if it had to happen at all. At least then the older ones wouldn't have been able to understand what was going on. It's embarrassing for them. Imagine, at their ages, having your friends and strangers ask you about your parents going to prison. People are so fucking rude, especially on the Internet. They don't even stop to think about how their words might hurt my girls. They just hide behind their computer screens and write whatever they want without even knowing us. My daughters are extremely resilient—they've had to be—but they're still kids. Even Gia. They didn't deserve any of this. And I hate the fact that they've had to endure so much, even more than I hated being in prison. And prison is no walk in the park, believe me.

Joe can't stand being in there any more than I could, but

I'm sure he'll be fine. He works out a lot, which is good. He also takes classes, because he dropped out of high school and even though he earned his GED, for some strange reason we can't find his diploma. So I said to him, "Who cares? You have nothing in there but time. Do it again." I'm very into school now. I think it's so important to graduate from high school and college. Back when Joe was in high school, it wasn't that big of a thing. He was really successful, so he struck out on his own. That's what turned me on to him in the first place. He owned two homes and worked really hard. I tell my daughters, "Make sure you marry a guy who goes to school and has a strong work ethic."

When Joe comes out, I want him to have a fresh start. I want him to look good, to feel good, and to stay on the straight and narrow and get a job. I don't know if he'll be able to go back to construction or if he even wants to, but he definitely needs to start working again and make money, so everything won't be on me. I just get anxious about it. That's what I think about when I can't sleep at night. I say to myself, *Oh my God, it's like we're starting all over.* That's what bothers me. It better happen right away, because it's a lot to handle on my own. I want to have faith in him because, like I said, at one point he was really successful, and everybody looked up to him. Then I don't know what happened. The economy crashed, and I think it took a toll on him. I just didn't know it at the time.

He's not the kind of guy to walk around depressed. He's always happy, happy, happy, at least on the outside. That was another thing I loved about him. He had such a positive out-look on life. He was always trying to come up with ideas for new business ventures. He says he can't wait to come out and start working. And I say, "Yeah, you better!" I'm not kidding. He better get his ass in gear on day one. Maybe he'll write a book about his experience. He remembers everything; way more than I do, so I could see him doing that.

Frankly, I don't care what the hell he does, as long as he does something, and that something makes a lot of money.

I don't want to have to worry or shoulder the burden of be-ing the sole breadwinner anymore.

I'm so over it.

18

MY GIRLS

As a result of the mistakes Joe made, I always tell my daughters, "Even if you marry a rich guy, you need to know that you can support yourself if things don't work out the way you expected." I learned that the hard way, and I don't want them to have to do the same. I have very high hopes for my girls, and they have high hopes for themselves, too, which makes me extremely proud. They're all smart, motivated, and mature beyond their years.

Gia says she wants to get into law. She's not sure exactly which area of the field she's interested in yet, but she says her desire stems from everything we've been through and all of the injustices we've been forced to tolerate. I'm sure she wants to help people like us. People who got in trouble but didn't know they were doing anything wrong. Well, at least I didn't. And, if that's one positive thing that comes out of all of this, I'll be thrilled. I'd love to have a lawyer in the family—in whatever capacity it ends up being! Everyone says how intelligent and responsible she is. I have to say they all are. But, if I'm being honest, Gia is the best at arguing her point. It's almost impossible to say no to her! That may be because she's the oldest, although she's always been very articulate and into her studies. She's so thorough when she's doing her homework and stuff like that, and I know you have to be able to concentrate and work really hard in order to pass the bar exam and practice law.

We have a few friends who are lawyers who've offered to let her shadow them for a day or two to see what she's most interested in pursuing. Then maybe she can do an internship to really narrow it down. She's also very into forensics, which I think is so fascinating. I'm not entirely sure where that came from, but she does watch those crime dramas on television sometimes. Recently she was watching that show *Prison Break* and she was totally into it. Then she got Milania into it, too, and Gia was getting annoyed at her because Milania was trying to tell her what happened and Gia didn't want to know the ending until she saw it herself! Sisters will be sisters!

If you ask me, I think Gia will get married, have kids, and have a very successful career, in whatever field that ends up being. If it's law, that's great. If it's forensics, that's great, too. I don't care what it is. I just want her to enjoy life. I think that's what every parent wants for their kids.

Gabriella also has a great head on her shoulders and she's very athletic. She tells me often that she wants to be a professional soccer player. How amazing would that be? I go to her games all the time, and she's really talented. She's so driven. She plays forward, and when I watch her, I can tell that in addition to being strong physically, her mind is always on the game. She's always calculating her next move before she makes it, which I think is a big part of being a professional athlete and a big part of being successful in general. This season, she asked to switch soccer teams because she felt like she wasn't reaching her full potential. She thought she wasn't being challenged enough. Isn't that awesome that she recognized that on her own? She knows what she wants and she goes after it. Even her coach says how much he loves her and how determined she is. I'm so impressed!

Gabriella brings this enormous energy to everything she does. She's a hard worker and she's at her best when she's being challenged. I can tell that she doesn't just do something because she enjoys it; she does it to get better at it. She's constantly trying to improve her skills, which I admire. She has this unbelievable passion for the game; she says it makes her feel powerful when she's out there on the field doing her thing. I love, love, love that! Feeling powerful is so important, especially as a woman.

In addition to being a soccer star, Gabriella is also a phenomenal writer. She's even in honors writing at school. Who knows, maybe she'll combine the two and become a sports reporter. I've heard they need smart, outgoing women in that line of work. That would be so great because she loves sports and she's confident in front of an audience. In fact, just the other day, these people came to her school to tell their stories about what happens when you text and drive. One of them had lost their parents that way. The teacher asked Gabriella if she would be interviewed by the reporter who was there to cover the story because she's very well spoken, just like Gia.

Of course the craziest one is Milania; she always makes us laugh. I could totally see Milania on TV in some capacity. She keeps telling me she wants to be in the movies. Can you imagine? I can! She loves to act, even though she thinks she's a terrible singer (she's not!). I'm going to sign her up for performing arts classes in the fall. She has the personality for the small and big screen, but she definitely needs a little training if she's serious about chasing that dream. She said to me the other day, "You know being in the movies is hard. You don't just become a star overnight. It may never happen." But I tell her she can't think that way. If you want to make something happen you have to think affirmative thoughts and you have to roll up your sleeves and put the time in. That's what I do every day.

I actually took her for an audition a while back and I think she got discouraged because the casting director wanted her to read the script a certain way and that wasn't the way she read it. She didn't know exactly what to do because no one's ever told her. But when you go to acting school, they teach you how to read. One of her friends just got a commercial after going to the performing arts school for five years. It just takes patience and practice. For example, I had a part in a recent production of *The Vagina Monologues* at the Andiamo Celebrity Showroom in Warren, Michigan, and I had a coach who helped me. He told me things like which lines and sections to emphasize and so on. I really listened to his suggestions, and everybody said I rocked it. I know Milania will be able to do the same. She's outgoing and poised, just like her mom!

And if acting doesn't work out, Milania is interested in the law as well—same as Gia—she wants to help people with their problems. My kids are like that. They're very compassionate.

As for Audriana, she's only seven, but she says she wants to be a contortionist! I didn't even know she knew that word. She loves dancing and gymnastics and all that kind of stuff, so anything is possible! As soon as she got into it, we knew she'd found her calling. In addition to doing dancing and gymnastics as extracurricular activities, she practices around the house and in the backyard all the time! Sometimes, out of the corner of my eye, I'll see her do a cartwheel in the living room! I just bought her a gym mat and this big roll thing that she can use to improve her back handsprings. She's totally into it, and she's so good! I can't believe how flexible she is. Even with all my yoga, I'm not that flexible. Maybe one day!

Toward the end of the school year, they did this "wax museum" project. The idea was that everyone had to pick someone they wanted to grow up to be like, and replicate that person. They had to dress like them and write an autobiography, as if they were that person, and then present it in the cafeteria in front of an audience. As soon as she got the assignment, Audriana immediately said she wanted to be the gymnast Laurie Hernandez. Laurie was part of the US women's gymnastics team that won the gold medal in the 2016 Summer Olympics. And she also got a silver medal on the balance beam. Once Audriana had decided on Laurie, I went out and bought her a book about her and she dressed up in a leotard for her performance. It was so cute!

I also spoke to her teacher that day, who said that sometimes Audriana will just be sitting in class and all of a sudden one of her legs or feet will fly up in the air. Isn't that so funny? She practices in the middle of school without even being aware of it! That shows me how passionate and dedicated she is.

Honestly, all my girls are that way. And I want them to pursue their dreams, no matter what they are. I'll be supportive of them in every single one of their endeavors.

Naturally, I would love for them to go to college. To me, that's very important. Listen, I know you can make money without it, but I just think it's a very competitive world we live in. And I want them to go to good colleges, so they can get a well-rounded education. It's something that they need in their lives. I would even be okay with them going to a university farther away from home for the experience, because I wasn't allowed to do that. My dad was very strict with me, so I ended up getting my associate's degree in fashion and marketing management from Berkeley College in New Jersey, but I'm not as protective of my kids as my father was with me. I want them to spread their wings and fly. I know they can do whatever they set their minds to. As I said, if they want to marry rich men, great! But even if their husbands have all the money in the world, I want them to have something that defines them. Something that makes them their own individuals and makes them interesting.

I'm sure they're going to lead very happy, full lives. I just hope that after college they always stay close by, because we're very into family. I would love to all move to California together one day. I really would. I'm not kidding. That's *my* dream.

What? I hear surfing gives you great abs!

19

.

WHAT LIES AHEAD

These days, I spend a lot of time thinking about where I came from, how much I've endured, and what my life is going to be like moving forward. I often wonder to myself what life would be like if I'd taken a different turn at some point in the road. What if I'd made a different decision? What if I'd never listened to Joe and been naive enough to believe that the choices he made were smart? Because they weren't. They were stupid. And, as I said, I'm pissed as hell.

Looking back, I realize that there were a lot of things that Joe did that weren't right. I've never told anyone this, but before we had Audriana—our fourth daughter—Joe and I did in vitro fertilization with the intent of gender selection, in order to try for a son. It seems like another lifetime ago, but it's true.

Joe came to me one day, out of the blue, and said, "I'd like to see if we can have a boy. Isn't there a way to do that?" Of course he loved our daughters beyond anything, but I guess he'd read something about it or seen something on TV and figured, why not give it a shot, with so much modern technology out there that makes it feasible.

I was definitely shocked and not sure what to say at first. I'd never had trouble getting pregnant the natural way, so I wondered whether it was right to try to control the process, if it wasn't absolutely necessary. It seemed like trying to play God for no good reason. I'd also heard that going through IVF was extremely difficult, with all of the shots and hormones and then the retrieval and transfer. I wasn't sure if I wanted to put my body through something that strenuous if I didn't have to.

Still, I knew I wanted a fourth child. I felt like three was an uneven number. I assumed that when they got older it might be harder for three of them to get together, so it would be nice to have two and two. Also, with three, two can gang up on the other one! So there was that. But still.

I thought about it for a long while. I weighed the pros and cons. Then, eventually, I said to myself, if this is something my husband really wants, then I should at least try it for him. Right? That's what spouses do for each other. They sacrifice to make the other one happy.

So, a few weeks later, I went to my gynecologist and asked if she could recommend a fertility specialist in New Jersey. She was pretty confused initially, because I was so fertile on my own, but I explained to her how Joe was feeling and that I wanted to be able to give him a son if that was what he wanted. She understood that and said she'd find the right person for us, which she did.

It was a very intense process, as millions of women already know. It really messed with my body and made me gain a lot of weight, which I was not thrilled about. First, they had to make sure I was at the right point in my menstrual cycle before we could even begin. There were tons of doctor's visits, which meant ultrasounds and having my blood drawn *constantly*. I also had to administer dozens of shots to myself, which I'd never done before. Those made my hormone levels go crazy. Then I had to do the final injection—called HCG. The timing of that is so specific. They monitor you with more ultrasounds and then tell you the exact hour to do it. If the shot is given too early, the eggs will not be mature enough. If it's given too late, the eggs may be too ripe and won't fertilize properly. I couldn't believe it. It was all very stressful. I see why people do it when they can't get pregnant on their own, but in our case it seemed excessive. Having sex is much easier!! Still, I kept thinking if it'll make Joe happy, then it'll make me happy.

Finally, once all that was done, they took the eggs out of me and then Joe did his thing so they could get a sperm sample and complete the fertilization process before weeding out the boys and implanting them into my uterus. I didn't understand exactly how all that worked, but we decided to put three eggs in. I remember the doctor saying, "You know you could have twins or triplets." And I said, "No, I just want one!" But we knew the odds would be better if we went with three, so we took a chance. Can you imagine if we'd had six kids?! Three girls and three boys! That would have been insane. And I'd be even more irritated at Joe now if I had to deal with all that by myself.

Unfortunately, in the end, it didn't work. We didn't even get one egg that took. I was disappointed, because I'd been through so much for no reason, and because it was so expensive. Joe was ticked off that I didn't get pregnant. He said, "You never had a problem before. I can't believe you did all this and we paid so much for nothing." He felt like he'd been ripped off. He didn't like being told that he still owed money but had nothing to show for it. That's how Joe is. He lets his frustration get in the way of common sense. The fact is, it doesn't matter whether it works. You're still responsible for the balance.

So this is where Joe got stupid. The same way he did with our taxes. He refused to give the outstanding ten thousand dollars we owed to the fertility clinic, simply because he didn't want to pay them. And because he felt wronged. The thing is, you can't do that. You can't act that way! He should have known that. He should have behaved like a grown-up. I wanted to just pay them and get it over with. But I didn't have a leg to stand on back then because it was before the show and I didn't have a salary of my own. Joe said to me, "Listen to your husband." So just like when he asked me to sign those tax documents, I did.

And guess what happened? The fertility clinic put a lien on our house. Yup, that's right.

So, again, I said to him, "Just pay them!" I didn't give a shit about the money, because—for whatever reason—I didn't want anyone to find out we'd done IVF in the first place. I don't know why I felt that way. Now, in retrospect, I'm glad I'm finally talking about it.

For the record, I paid the money back when I got home from prison. I just wanted to move on and clean everything up. I wanted everything to be good.

Of course Joe and I went on to have a fourth child anyway—the good old-fashioned way—and it was another girl! Our sweet Audriana. Thank God the in vitro didn't work, because then we may never have had her. Life has a funny way of working out like that. And now we're so done! I'm happy with my four daughters.

But I'm still not happy with Joe. Actually, that's the understatement of the friggin' century. And I'm not going to hide it anymore. It took me a while to get here. At first, I tried to cover for him. I tried to believe that he had no idea what he was doing. That's what I would tell anyone who asked. I loved my husband. I stood behind him and supported him. I thought, *Why would he lie? Why would he do something so blatantly wrong?* And, most important, why the fuck would he drag me down with him?! Did he think we were invincible? Again, just stupid decision making on his part, and I have no more patience for stupidity anymore.

I just can't ignore the truth. Not when it's staring me right in the face.

I used to lead a charmed life. Joe made plenty of money to support our family and then some. I didn't have to work at all. I could go shopping whenever I wanted. There were plenty of times when I spent upward of ten thousand dollars on clothing and accessories for myself and the girls without batting an eyelash. I didn't have a worry in the world. I also had a husband at home to help out with things, even though most of the domestic responsibilities were mine. I didn't care! I had nothing else to do except take care of my kids, do the errands, and cook dinner every night. I was happy and relaxed.

Until Joe fucked up. And he fucked up bad.

After that, life became very different.

Now I'm a single mother. I handle everything. All of it. And I support my entire family financially, which is a big weight on my shoulders on top of everything else.

I take all four kids to school every day, which means making lunches, and driving back and forth, since they're at different schools. I sign them up for and bring them to all their activities, help with homework, and cook dinner. I go to the supermarket and the dry cleaner and run a long list of other errands. There's always something! I make sure that the girls have what they need in the way of clothing and sports equipment. I'm a 24-7 mom. I also work, pay the bills, and handle everything for the house. I do have a cleaning lady every other week, but when you have a ten-thousand-plus-square-foot home, four acres of land, four kids, and dogs, that's not enough! So I'm also the backup housekeeper. I'm literally wiping down countertops all day long! It never ends.

Not to mention that I'm also handling the stuff Joe used to do. Every week there's something that goes wrong in our house. We've been living here coming up on ten years, so things are falling apart left and right. The gate just broke, so I had to call someone to come fix that. Every winter the columns start deteriorating and we have to re-cement them. The landscaping needs work. The garage opener on the wall, where you punch in the code, just fell down, so now I have to deal with that. And the other day I had to call the electrician for some other issues. It's constant.

And don't even get me started on the laundry. I'm scared to count the number of loads I do every week! I will say that my kids are amazing. They pitch in as much as they can, even though they're so busy with school and extracurricular activities. I taught them all how to do laundry. Gabriella learned when I got home, and Gia took on some of it while I was away, even though my mom was also around and she did most of it. She was an enormous help to Joe. I only wish she could be here for me, too.

Listen, I deal with everything. I'm strong like that. And I know there are a lot of other women out there who do the same stuff that I do and then some. I salute them. I really do. But it doesn't change the fact that I resent it, because for me, it didn't have to be this way.

I also resent the fact that Joe being gone puts a lot more pressure on my kids. That makes me feel badly for them and angry at Joe. I mean, yes, the girls are fantastic and have been so tough in the face of so much adversity, but why should they have to pick up his slack? Why should their lives have to be affected by what their father did?

For example, when I was in Italy and my father was in the hospital that whole week, Gia had to step up in a major way. Gabriella, too. They all had to help out because I couldn't be there. I had to work. So all of a sudden they have this huge responsibility when they shouldn't. They're kids. They don't need all that added pressure on them. I want them to enjoy their lives. I don't want Gia to feel accountable for staying home alone at night with her sisters. I don't want Gabriella to have to wake up in the morning and make breakfast for everyone. Or for either of them to have to help the younger girls with homework when they already have so much of their own. Sure, I think my daughters should do chores around the house and learn to be capable adults who appreciate all that they have.

But this is just too much.

And, believe me, I give Joe plenty of attitude about it. No more playing the supportive wife. Some days when I talk to him I'm in a good mood, some days I'm in a cranky mood. It depends how my day is going. Joe gets it. Or at least I hope he does.

He's always saying things like, "Honey, I'm so sorry. When I come home, I will do everything you're doing now. You won't have to do anything. I will drive the kids everywhere."

Blah, blah, blah. I'll believe it when I see it.

It's not that I think he doesn't mean what he's saying. I do. It's just a long time until he comes home, and actions speak much louder than words. He claims he's working on himself so that he can be a better husband. He says he's going to appreciate me more like he did when I got home.

I sure hope so, because if he doesn't, I'm not sure what will happen. I guess I'm going to cross that bridge when I get to it. I'd like to think he won't be the same person as he was before. There's just no way that he won't change. I mean, all you do in prison is think about how to improve yourself. I'm definitely not the same person I was before I was incarcerated.

My kids know I'm frustrated with their father. I can't hide that, nor would I want to. They hear me talking to him and snapping at him sometimes. I just tell them, "Listen, nothing is guaranteed in life. I don't know what's going to happen with me and Daddy. I'm just living day by day." And, for now, I'm waiting for their father, because I'm not going to divorce him while he's locked up.

But, to tell you the truth, I don't know what's going to happen. I mean, do I see Joe and me together in ten years? Do I see us growing old together? I don't know. Maybe. Maybe not. He'll always be a part of my life, because he's the father of my children; that I can say for sure. You just never know what's going to happen. I never thought I would lose my mother when she was only sixty-six years old. Life is a roller coaster, and you have to ride the highs and the lows all the same.

What I do know about my life in ten, twenty, thirty years is that I'll have my kids beside me. And given that, I'll have found the root of my happiness. My daughters are everything to me. That will never change.

Just the other day, this woman who lives in my town came up to me at a restaurant and said, "I wanted to tell you how sorry I am about your mom." Then she told me that she understood what I was going through because she'd just lost her son at nineteen years old. Can you imagine that? Nineteen! He hadn't even lived his life yet. I was so sad for her. I've always been the mom who said if anything ever happened to my kids, I would die right along with them. I also said if anything ever happened to my parents, I'd die with them, too. And then look what happened. I'm still here. Some days are hard—unbearable, even—but I'm still standing.

My point is that life is short and we never know what tomorrow will bring. Never in a million years did I think I'd be experiencing such profound emptiness. My mother was the only person I could depend on when everyone else depends on me. I used to talk to her about everything. And while I can and do talk to my dad now that she's gone, it's not exactly the same. I used to go deeper with her. That's the relationship of a mother and daughter—at least that was our relationship. I confided in her about Joe all the time and how furious I was.

She would just say, "Whatever makes you happy. I will stand by you no matter what. I just want you to be happy and at peace." My dad says the same thing. It's rare to have a marriage like theirs and still be so in love almost half a century later!

No one in our family has ever gotten divorced. But my parents both said they'd be fine with it if I decide to leave Joe. They feel like I didn't deserve what happened to me. They definitely feel like Joe is to blame, but—again—they never said a bad thing about him. I think that's beyond amazing, especially because Joe's mother called me a bitch and blamed me for the whole thing. Trust me, my parents could have ripped into him because it was all his doing. But they never did, despite the fact that he left me with four kids and a mountain of debt.

I had to pay restitution. I paid off all the bankruptcy stuff, since we ended up withdrawing from filing. And I still have taxes to pay. I'm always worrying about making sure I can support my family. I'm counting on the fact that there will be a season nine of *Real Housewives*, but nothing is guaranteed in this world. I need the show to stay afloat while I broaden the rest of my career.

Unfortunately, Joe can't make any money while he's in prison, and who knows what he'll do when he gets out. I don't know if he can go back to construction. He has to earn people's trust again. He has to figure that all out. Because, I'll tell you one thing, he is *not* going to sit at home and do nothing. Or just play Mr. Mom. He needs to get to work and support his family *without* evading his taxes. He says he's thinking while he's in prison about what he's going to do to make money when he gets out. He asked me to trademark some "wine in a can" thing the other day. Who knows if that will ever come to fruition, but I'm trying to get him a patent in case it does. I hope he finds something to succeed at. For his benefit and my benefit, yes, but mostly for our kids. They deserve the world, and Joe needs to help me give them that.

I never thought I'd be a single mother. I never thought I'd be the sole breadwinner for our family. I didn't sign up for this.

Yet here I am. And it's a lot.

Still, I'm keeping my head above water. I'm killing myself every day to do that. I won't give up.

I'm standing strong.

ACKNOWLEDGMENTS

FROM TERESA GIUDICE:

I would like to thank God for blessing me with the will and strength to stand strong during this very challenging year.

La Familia

I would like to thank my Papa, Giacinto Gorga, for everything you have shown me and taught me since I was a little girl. I would not be here if you did not show me the way.

To my four babies, Gia, Gabriella, Milania, and Audriana: Everything I do, I do for each one of you.

To my husband, Joe, I wish you were home and can't wait until you are.

To my brother, Joey; Melissa; and to my husband's family, thank you for all of the love and support you continue to show for my daughters.

Miei amici

Rosana Harms, Lisa Giammarino, Lisa Fortunato, Dina Manzo, John and Kim Raciopi, Dana Levine, Siggy Flicker, Dolores Catania, Dana Torsiello, and anyone I may have missed, thank you for being there for me and my family through all of the ups and downs. May god bless all of you and your families.

La Mia Squadra

To Priscilla DiStasio, my very talented make-up artist, thank you for your loyalty, your amazing work, and your friendship.

To Jim Leonard, my attorney and very dear friend, for always telling me what I need to hear, even when I don't want to hear it. Also, to Rebecca and everyone at Leonard Law Group, thank you for everything.

To David Antunes and Lucia Casazza, my two hair stylists, thank you for your amazing work and for always being there when I need you.

To Karianne Fischbach, thank you for handling my appearances and making sure everything runs smoothly. Thank you for everything you do.

To Carolos Cuevas and Anthony Rainone, thank you for everything you have done.

Televisione

To Frances Berwick, Shari Levine, Andy Cohen, everyone at Bravo, Lucilla D'Agostino, Dorothy Toran, everyone at Sirens Media/LeftField, thank you for putting up with me for the last nine years . . . here is to nine more.

Libro

To Louise Burke, the amazing Jen Bergstrom, Frank Weimann, Nina Cordes (I miss you already), Jennifer Robinson, John Vairo, Laura Waters, everyone at Simon & Schuster/Gallery Books, and everyone at Folio Literary Management, for giving my literary endeavors a home and allowing me to be me. PS: get ready for a spicy fiction series. . . . You never saw my third Danbury diary . . .

To Emily Liebert, thank you for helping me organize my thoughts for this book, you were amazing to work with. Thank you.

Media

To KC Baker, my friend and coauthor on *Turning The Tables*, Charlotte Triggs, Emily Strohm, everyone at *People*, Jennifer Peros, Carolyn Greenspan Rosen, everyone at *Entertainment Tonight*, AJ Calloway, super-producer Darius Brown, everyone at *Extra*, Amy Robach, Katie Conway, everyone at *Good Morning America*, Beth Sobol, everyone at *E! News*, the amazing Dr. Oz, thank you all for being so fair to me over the years.

Last, but not least, to the *Real Housewives* fans out there, especially the RHONJ fans, thank you for all of your support over the years, I love, love, love and appreciate each and every one of you, even the haters.

xo

Teresa

2017